How to Make Adorable

Baby
Animal Dolls

With Soft-Sculpted Bodies
and Heads Made with
Silky-Smooth Home-Made Air-Dry Clay

By Jonni Good

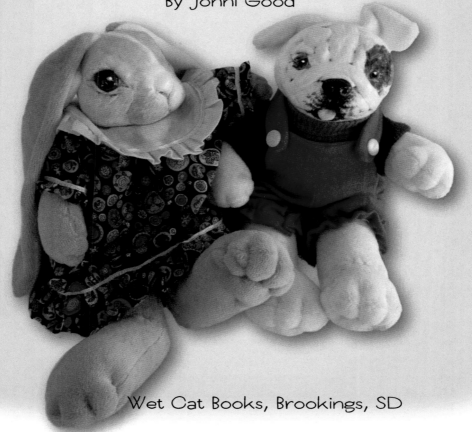

Wet Cat Books, Brookings, SD

Text and illustrations © 2013 Jonni Good

Wet Cat Books
909 3rd Street
Brookings, SD 57006
www.WetCatBooks.com
Printed in USA

ISBN 978-0-9741065-7-1

More Books by Jonni Good:

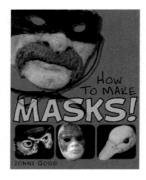

Contents:

Introduction

A few days ago my 6-year old grandson asked me why I was writing a doll book. I told him it's because I like teaching people how to do things that make them happy—and these dolls can actually make you happy twice! First, there's the creative enjoyment that comes from making the dolls themselves, using simple techniques and inexpensive materials. Then, if you can bear to part with your doll after you make it, you can make someone else happy when they receive your handmade collector's doll as a gift. With such sweet faces and toes, who could not fall instantly in love?

In this book I show you exactly how to make your own adorable baby animal dolls, leading you through the entire process every step of the way. Your dolls won't cost much to make, and every doll will be an original, one-of-a-kind work of art. Since no two dolls ever come out exactly alike, each doll will have it's own personality and character.

You won't have to learn how to make molds for the doll heads, because each one is hand-sculpted over a simple armature that you make with a baby sock filled with rice or kitty litter. You don't need a kiln, because you'll be using home-made air-dry clay instead of porcelain. The bodies and ears are made out of soft, huggable cotton velour, and the toes are sculpted with a few easy stitches.

A Bit of History . . .

I came up with the basic design for these dolls back in the late 1980's, when I sold them at the Saturday Market in Portland, Oregon. The dolls were fun to make, and I felt like I was giving my customers something really special that they couldn't get anywhere else.

After a reporter found my dolls at the market and ran a story in a national magazine, I received orders from gift shops all around the country. I couldn't make dolls fast enough to fill all the orders myself, so my parents volunteered to help out. My mom sewed the bodies and clothes (she even knitted some tiny sweaters for them). My father worked on the heads. That led to another media event, when the Bellingham Herald ran a big article about my dad, with photos of "the retired pile driver with reptile tattoos on his forearms" surrounded by a table full of his hand-painted doll heads. (You can see a recent picture of my dad, with dolls he designed himself, on page 3.)

Our dolls were accepted into some of the most exclusive arts and craft shows in the Pacific Northwest.

The original dolls were made with soft cotton velour, just like the ones you'll make with the patterns included in this book. My father still had the patterns stashed away in a cupboard, and I was able to use them in this book with very few changes.

However, the heads are now much easier to make. Our original method was just too complicated, and most people who tried to make them the old way couldn't get them to come out right.

Since the original technique was so difficult to learn how to do, I didn't feel that I could write a book about them—until now. Two things had to happen first:

The first breakthrough happened when Barbara Bell, a doll-maker from Kingsport, TN, wrote a guest post for my blog titled "How to Make an Armature for Doll Heads and Puppets." She described a method for making hollow puppet and doll heads without a seam by "by sewing a small fabric bag and firmly filling it with clean cat litter clay granules." She found the idea in an out-of-print book called "The Complete Encyclopedia of Crafts," published in 1975 by Columbia House. Another reader pointed out that a similar method is used by Susanna Oroyan, which she describes in detail in her book "Designing the Doll." These simple armatures allow us to make hollow, seamless doll heads, without using a mold.

The second breakthrough came when I made a few changes to my original paper mache clay recipe, which was featured in my book titled "Make Animal Sculptures with Paper Mache Clay." Thousands of people have now used the original recipe to make beautiful sculptures. (You would not believe how much easier it is to use than the old traditional paper strips and paste!)

For the small, highly-detailed dolls, I wanted a sculpting material that worked a bit more like some of the commercial air-dry clays. After spending several weeks experimenting and tinkering with that original recipe in my kitchen, the new air-dry clay recipe was born. It became an instant hit as soon as I posted the new recipe on my blog and YouTube channel. Doll-makers have been especially excited about it, because it reminds them of Creative PaperClay™, but it's much less expensive.

The new air-dry clay dries somewhat softer than the original paper mache clay, so it's easier to sand. It contains less paper, so it's smoother and easier to sculpt into tiny details. You can get the surface as smooth as porcelain, if that's the look you're after. (In fact, several of my readers thought we should call it "paper porcelain").

When the new air-dry clay is formed over plaster cloth, as you'll be doing for your armatures, the result is surprisingly strong and durable. I discovered exactly how strong it can be when I tried out the brand new recipe to make the Indian Rhino sculpture you see in the photo. It was made with two layers of plaster cloth covered with a thin layer of air-dry clay, exactly the same way the doll heads are made (although the armature was made with pottery clay instead of a baby sock). And, just like the doll heads, the rhino sculpture is hollow. (The rhino's friend and fellow puppy-sitter, the giraffe, was made with traditional paper mache using paper strips and paste.)

Once I realized that the dolls could be made in a new, easier way, I knew it was time to write this book.

Soft Sculpting and Sewing

The combination of hard and soft materials is one of the reasons why these dolls are so much fun to make. You work for a while with air-dry clay and acrylic paint, creating the adorable doll heads. Then you move on to sewing and sculpting the soft cotton velour bodies. And after that, you get to pick out fabrics and lace and ribbons for a dress or playsuit. All you need is a "fat quarter" of material to make a doll or dress, so all this creativity doesn't come with a high price tag—but the results, as they say, are priceless!

I freely admit that I'm not a master seamstress, and the patterns in this book were designed with my limited sewing skills in mind. That means that just about anyone can sew the bodies and clothes in this book. In fact, the dolls are small enough that you could sew them by hand instead of using a sewing machine, if you want to.

However, if you have never sewn anything before, or if your sewing skills are getting a bit rusty, I suggest that you find a good basic sewing book at your local library. The instructions in this book do assume that you have some familiarity with a few of the more common sewing terms.

Get Creative . . .

Remember that kittens, bunnies and puppies come in hundreds of different colors and coat patterns, and I couldn't possibly include all those variations in this book. That doesn't mean that you can't make them yourself, though. Just do a Google image search to find models for your dolls.

You can even make portrait dolls, using your own favorite animal for the model, like I did when I used a baby photo of my cat to make my ragdoll kitten doll, shown above.

If you want a bigger doll, you can do that, too, like my dad did when he designed his giant rabbit and cat dolls. (That's my dad, Pete Havekost, in the photo on the left.) He made his dolls large enough so he could dress them in baby clothes from the local thrift store. To make them bigger, use adult socks or a sewn cloth bag instead of baby socks for your head armature, and then draw your body patterns to fit the new head.

And remember that just because I couldn't find the space for a raccoon doll, or a mouse, that doesn't mean that you can't make one if you want to. As you'll quickly see, it would be easy to change the head armatures and use your air-dry clay to sculpt the face of a bear cub or a fox—or whatever baby animal you happen to love most. You wouldn't even have to change the body pattern for most species, although monkeys and apes would need hands instead of paws.

In fact, as I proved with the Indian Rhino, you can use the air-dry clay and plaster cloth to make lots of things besides dolls—once you get started, who knows what you'll create next?

Keep it Safe . . .

The dolls in this book should be considered collector's dolls, not toys. Since the dolls are made with materials that we buy at the hardware store, I don't recommend giving the dolls to babies or small children. The air-dry clay has not been tested for safety, many acrylic paints contain pigments that you wouldn't want a baby to eat, and the clothes might be made with buttons or other small things that could choke a baby. Besides, the finished dolls are original works of art, so they really should really be given to someone who's old enough to appreciate their unique qualities.

Be sure to read the labels on the products used to make the clay, and wear a mask if you need to sand the head. Keep the unused clay away from young kids, because it looks a lot like cookie dough, and you don't want them to eat the stuff.

If you have any questions about the process, or if you'd like to share a photo of your finished dolls, be sure to come visit me on my blog at UltimatePaperMache.com. I love answering questions, and I love to learn from my readers. I hope to see you there, soon.

Air-Dry Clay Recipe

About the Clay:

As soon as I developed this recipe, I published it on my blog and on my YouTube channel. A lot of my regular readers tried it out on their own sculptures, and the response has been overwhelmingly positive.

Many people agree that it is very similar to working with Creative Paperclay®, but it's much less expensive.

Some of the products in the recipe, like the drylwall joint compound, are normally sold in gallon-sized containers that will make many batches of clay. For that reason, if you only want to make one doll. you may want to use Creative Paperclay instead of making your own. However, it's hard to imagine making just one. As soon as your friends and family see your first adorable doll, they'll want one, too.

One recipe will make enough clay for three or four doll heads. If you don't want to make several dolls at the same time, a tightly covered container or a plastic bag will keep it from drying out. To prevent the growth of mold, be sure to add the household bleach or oil of clove—it will help your clay stay usable longer.

I made all of the dolls in this book with the new air-dry clay recipe. If you use Creative Paperclay instead, be sure to read the instructions on the wrapper.

About the Ingredients:

You can find the ingredients for the air-dry clay at your local hardware store and grocery store. You'll be quite familiar with most of the

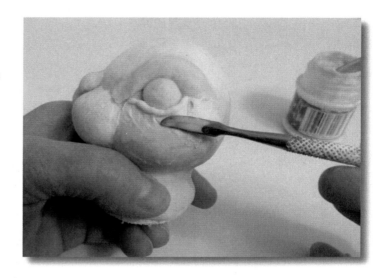

products in the recipe, because you probably use them all the time. However, the joint compound may be new to you if you don't do much home remodeling. It's a product used in the construction industry. You can buy a gallon of joint compound at Home Depot for less than $5. Some stores sell it in smaller containers.

When the Elmer's glue is combined with the joint compound, the resulting mix becomes very strong when dry. The other ingredients, like the corn starch and white flour, are used as fillers, and they to help make the clay nice and smooth. The toilet paper adds additional strength. Technically, this is a home-made air-dry cellulose-reinforced polymer clay.

Joint Compound -

If you've ever done any remodeling or if you've watched someone build a wall with plaster board or Sheetrock™, you're familiar with this product. You can find drywall joint compound at a hardware store, or in the paint department of Walmart. To see how it's normally used in the construction industry, do a search for joint compound on YouTube.

If you don't live in the United States, the guys at the hardware store will probably have a different name for this product. Many of my blog readers sent in suggestions when I asked them to tell me what joint compound is called in other countries. You can find these suggestions here:

http://UltimatePaperMache.com/the-joint-compound-problem

Joint compound is usually sold in one-gallon plastic tubs. You want the pre-mixed kind that already has water mixed in with it. Do not buy the powdered form, (it will say "quick set" on the label) which contains Portland cement.

Elmer's Glue-All -

This glue can be found in large containers at the hardware store, or in small (more expensive) containers almost everywhere else. You only need ½ cup for a batch of clay. If you don't live in the US, look for a white PVA glue. They're available almost everywhere.

Cornstarch -

This is the product you buy at the grocery store to thicken your gravy. It is also called cornflour or maize starch. This is not the same as corn meal, which is used to make corn bread or tortillas. Cornstarch is a very fine, silky powder.

Cornstarch makes our air-dry clay feel really smooth and soft.

All-purpose Flour -

This is the same white flour that you buy to make cookies. If you don't already have some in the kitchen, just buy the cheapest brand you can find.

Toilet Paper -

Use whatever brand you have on hand.

Mineral Oil -

The oil keeps the clay from drying out too quickly, and adds a nice feel to the finished clay. The easiest way to buy mineral oil is to get a bottle of baby oil, which is usually mineral oil with a small amount of fragrance. If you're allergic to mineral oil, you can use linseed oil instead, or any vegetable oil.

You'll Also Need:

Mixer with Dough Hooks -

The mixer will combine all the ingredients and break the paper apart into tiny threads, so your clay will be smooth and workable. If you don't have a mixer with dough hooks, you can mix the final portion of flour in by hand, like you would if you were making bread.

I recommend using a mixer dedicated to your craft projects, since many of the ingredients used in the clay recipe are not edible. If you don't have a mixer, you can get a small one for around $30, or find one at your local thrift store for much less.

If you don't have a mixer and only want to make one or two dolls, you will probably want to buy a package of Creative Paperclay to make your dolls, instead of using this recipe.

Large Bowl, Measuring Cup and Tablespoon -

For measuring and mixing your clay.

Plastic Bag or Container with Tight-Fitting Lid -

To keep your clay from drying out between work sessions. I like to use both, just to make sure the clay is protected from the drying air.

Air Dry Clay Recipe -

- ½ cup joint compound (200 grams)
- ½ cup Elmer's Glue-All™ (130 grams)
- ½ cup cornstarch (70 grams)
- ½ cup damp toilet paper (24 grams dry, 110 grams wet)
- 3 tablespoons mineral oil (32 grams)
- ½ teaspoon household bleach or a few drops of clove oil
- 1 cup (more or less) all-purpose flour (170 grams, total)

Step 1 - Measuring the Toilet Paper

It is much easier to get your clay to come out right every single time if you use the gram measurements in the ingredient list above, and then follow the instructions for weighing and mixing that begin at the bottom of page 9. If you don't have a small kitchen scale, use the instructions for measuring the toilet paper in a cup, starting below. The important thing to remember is that the paper must be soaked in the water to soften it, and most of the water then needs to be pressed out of the paper. However, if you press the paper too hard, it will form hard lumps that will not mix out, and your clay will be bumpy and hard to use.

You can see a video showing how to weigh and mix the clay at UltimatePaperMache.com/dolls

Cup Method:

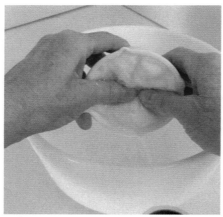

1. Take a handful of toilet paper off the roll and dip into warm water. Just get it wet, but not so soggy that it starts to fall apart.

2. Press the wet paper into a measuring cup, and squeeze out all the water.

3. After the water has been pressed out, check to see if the paper fills the measuring cup. If not, add more paper in the same way.

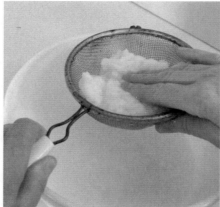

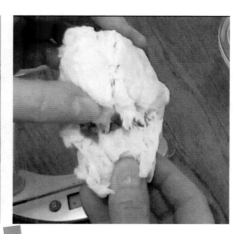

4. When you have ½ cup of damp paper, put it back into the warm water. Add the household bleach to the water. (Or use clove oil instead, and add it with the mineral oil in step 1, page 10. The bleach or clove oil prevent mold.)

5. Soak the paper for several minutes, then remove it from the water. A sieve helps, but is not necessary.

6. Press the water out of the paper, until you have a mass of damp, but not wet, paper pulp. Pour out the water.

Weight Method (Recommended):

1. Put your bowl on the scale, and hit the tare button to take the numbers to zero. Tear paper off the roll and add to the bowl until the weight is 24 grams

2. Add warm water to cover the paper, and allow it to soak for a few minutes.

3. Pour out the water and gently squeeze the water out of the paper. Continue to squeeze out water until the damp paper weighs 110 grams.

Step 2 - Mixing the Ingredients -

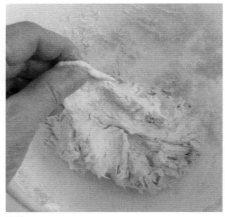
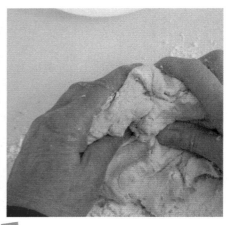

1. Put all of the first five ingredients in the bowl with the paper (add the clove oil if you didn't use bleach in the previous step). Add ½ cup (70 grams) of the all-purpose flour. Mix thoroughly with your electric mixer until the mixture is smooth and creamy. At this point, it will look a bit like a wet cookie dough.

2. Change to the dough hooks, and add the remaining flour, a little at a time, until the dough is well-mixed and it feels firm yet pliable. You should be able to form a thin pinch of clay without it sticking to your fingers.

3. Dust your work surface lightly with cornstarch, and knead the dough until it's smooth.

It should now be easy to form your clay into a very thin pancake, and you can roll it into a small ball or noodle. It will feel nice and silky, and should be only slightly tacky. If it still feels too wet, just dust on more cornstarch and knead again. If you add too much cornstarch and it gets too dry, knead in a very small dab of joint compound.

Store your finished clay in a covered bowl or plastic bag to keep it from drying out. It should last for at least a week if it is kept covered between work sessions.

Glue and Water Mixture –

In a small container with a tight-fitting lid, mix equal amounts of water and white glue (Elmer's Glue-All). You will use this mixture a lot when you sculpt your doll heads. It helps wet clay stick to a layer of dry clay underneath and it can also be used to help make the clay surface smooth.

There will be times when you want to limit the amount of glue and water mixture you use. When adding eyes, for instance, try to smooth the clay by patting it with a dry finger instead of rubbing with a damp finger. That way, the clay will dry faster, and you can work on the next feature more quickly.

Using the Glue and Water Mixture:

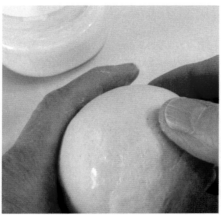

Before adding new clay to dried clay, brush on your glue mixture. This will make sure that the two layers bond together.

When you want the edge of new clay to mesh seamlessly with the dried clay beneath, use a bit of your glue mixture to soften the new clay and smooth the edge with your fingers or a sculpting tool.

To polish wet clay very smooth, dampen your finger or a soft brush with just enough glue mixture to let it slide smoothly over the clay. Then rub or brush until the clay is smooth.

Using Your Air-Dry Clay

Allow plenty of drying time -

I know you're in a real hurry to finish your doll, so you may be tempted to start sculpting and not stop until your head is completely done. I've tried this myself, and I always end up regretting it. The clay is fairly soft, so it's easy to damage a feature you just worked on if you don't give it a chance to at least develop a protective skin. Work on an area, then give it at least 20 minutes (preferably longer) to firm up. Then move on and do the next feature.

To make your clay dry faster -

Put your doll heads in front of a fan, or over a furnace vent where they will be hit with warm, moving air.

You can also dry them in an oven, at 250° F or lower. Do not "bake" the heads at a higher temperature, or they will darken, and you will smell burning glue in your kitchen.

If you're really in a hurry, find a warm spot and turn on the fan—it's quite a bit faster than baking them.

Make a drying rack -

If you only make one or two dolls, you don't need to make a special drying rack. You can set your doll heads on the neck of the bottle you use to make the armature (page 20) or just sit the dry bottom edge of the heads on a piece of foil or paper towel. However, if you want to make a lot of dolls, perhaps to give as gifts, a drying rack really helps.

I used a scrap of 1 x 8 pine, and screwed two scraps of 1 x 2 pine to it. Then I drilled holes slightly larger than my dowels (but stopping before drilling all the way through) and stuck my dowels in

the holes. Easy - it doesn't look great, but it's really handy.

Make good connections between bits of clay -

Be sure to use your glue and water mixture to make sure new clay is firmly attached to the dry clay underneath. Also, when putting two bits of new clay next to each other, smoosh the two wet edges together so there's no visible line between them. This helps make sure that the two pieces of clay will not pull apart when the head dries.

You may sometimes get small cracks or gaps when the clay dries, no matter how careful you are. Don't worry, though - this is really easy to fix.

How to repair boo-boos -

Sometimes gaps appear between pieces of clay, as shown below. And sometimes you just change your mind and decide you want a feature to be a different size, or you want a different expression.

It's easy to change a feature if it just needs to be a bit bigger. Brush on some of the glue and water mix to your dried doll head, add a bit of wet clay, and smooth it down all around the edges. It will dry a slightly different color than the clay underneath (I don't know why, but it won't matter—you'll be adding paint, anyway). The repair should be entirely invisible when the head is finished.

If the change you want requires the removal of dried clay, use a very sharp craft knife. You can also use a Dremel™ tool, if you have one. Cut away the extra clay, and sand the clay to make it smooth.

If the change would require cutting into the plaster cloth armature beneath the clay, you may be better off just starting over, However, if you're brave, go ahead and cut away the part you don't like, and add a piece of wet plaster cloth, preferably on the inside of the head. Allow it to harden in the shape you want, (you'll probably have to hold it for a few minutes while it hardens), and then cover with a thin layer of clay.

Repairing a small crack -

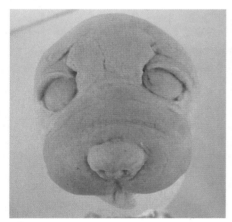 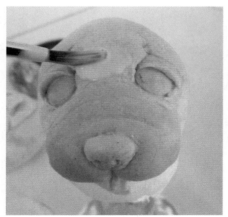 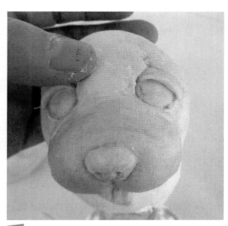

1. Take a close look at your doll's head after it's dry. If you see a gap or crack in the clay that doesn't add to the character of the doll, go ahead and fix it. In the photo above, you can see a small gap between the eyes.

2. Brush glue and water mixture over the area that needs to be repaired.

3. Press on a small amount of clay, and smooth it over the area with a finger dampened with the glue and water mixture.

Tools for Shaping Your Clay

I confess that I have a fairly large collection of modeling tools, but I use very few of them. In fact, for years the only tool I ever used to shape any kind of clay was a plain old table knife. (I still use it a lot when I'm working with pottery clay).

For the fine details on my doll heads, I like to use an inexpensive set of wax sculpting tools that I found on Amazon.com. I pick out a favorite tool, use it for everything until I lose it, and then pick out another one.

What this means, of course, is that you can use a tool that you already have on hand to shape your clay, as long as it is small enough to help you get the details you want. You can even make your own tools by whittling toothpicks, or get fancy and grind down a screwdriver. There's no need to spend a lot of money on tools for your air-dry clay.

For some features, the best tools are your dry fingers and hand. You can smooth the clay by patting it gently after it's been applied to the head. You can also shape the clay by rolling it around in the palm of your hand. Some artists like to roll out the air-dry clay between two pieces of plastic wrap before adding the first thin layer to their armatures, so it's an even thickness.

The small paint brush you use for the glue and water mixture can also be used to shape the clay, and to smooth and polish it after it's been applied to the head.

As you work with the clay, you'll develop methods that fit your own working style.

Painting Tips

You'll Need:

Acrylic Glazing Liquid

I use glazing liquid on many of my projects, because it helps bring out the sculpted details with very little work.

The glazing liquid lets you thin the consistency of your paint without adding water, so the paint becomes more transparent without getting drippy.

When the glazing liquid is added to paint, it allows you to work with the paint longer before it dries. When you use a dark brown paint with the glazing liquid and wipe most of it off, you end up with a slightly antiqued look that gives the doll head a nicely complex, interesting finish that high-lights the details. This is difficult to do without the glazing liquid, because acrylic paint dries so quickly.

I use the Golden brand acrylic glazing liquid. My local art supply store is very small and doesn't carry it, so I buy it online from DickBlick.com.

Acrylic Paint -

You can paint your doll heads with any acrylic artist's paint or craft paint. I particularly like the Golden Fluid Acrylics, but that's just a personal choice - use whichever brand you prefer.

Acrylic Gesso

Acrylic gesso will seal your doll head before painting it, and it will give it a nice white surface that really brings out the colors of the paint. I highly recommend using the acrylic gesso before painting your doll heads.

Satin or Matte Acrylic Varnish

After your doll's head has been painted and it's completely dry, you'll want to protect it with a coat of varnish, just as you would with any fine art. Any brand of acrylic varnish will work just fine.

Clear Fingernail Polish

The polish makes the doll's eyes bright and wet-looking. Use in a well-ventilated space - the fumes are deadly!

Painting Fur:

The only "rule" for painting the doll heads is to pick out the body fabric first. It is so much easier to match paint colors to fabric, than doing it the other way around.

This is how I painted all the doll heads in this book:

1. First, the head is sealed with Acrylic Gesso, which gives you a nice white surface to paint. Allow it to dry.

2. Next, a base coat is applied. This is usually the lightest color on the face. For the calico kitten in the photos, the base coat was a warm white, made with Titanium White and a tiny dab of Yellow Ochre. Allow the base coat to dry.

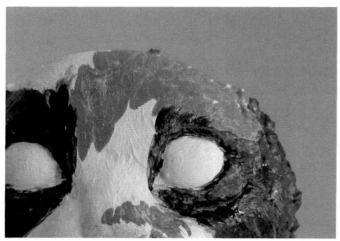

3. Spots are painted over the base coat, using the lightest color in the spots. Here, I used orange and a dark brown that was made very transparent by mixing with water.

4. Now that the basic color patterns have been established, we start to add fur marks, using colors that are just slightly darker or lighter than the base coat. Let the base coat show through between your brush marks, and continue to add layers of slightly differently colored fur until you have a coat that looks interesting and realistic.

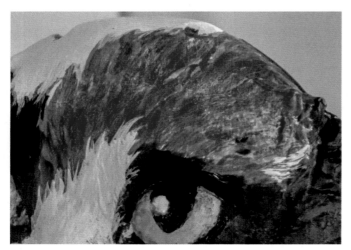

This system helps you match the heads to the body fabric, and it also gives you a lot of interesting and subtle color variations, like real fur.

Painting Eyes:

Light-Colored Eyes (Kittens, Blue-Eyed Bunny) -

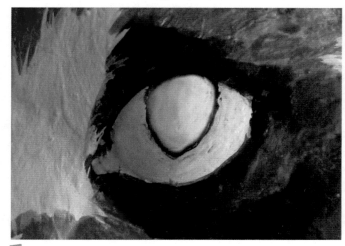

1. Mark the pupil with a pencil or permanent black marker, as shown here. Add a speck of light pink in the corner of the eye.

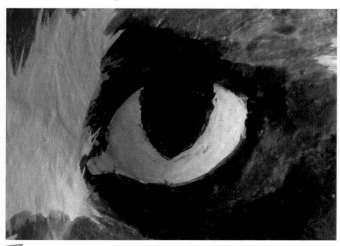

2. Then fill in the black pupil with acrylic paint. Allow this to dry completely before continuing with the colored iris.

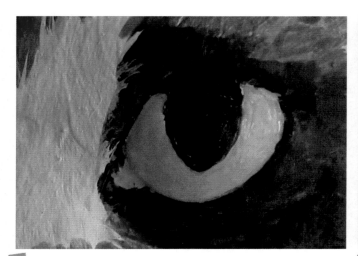

3. Choose the lightest color in the eye, and paint it over the iris. Allow it to dry

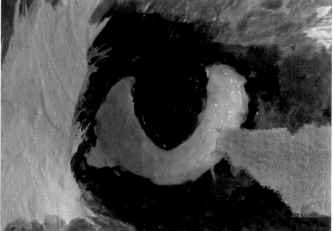

4. Choose the darkest color in the eye, and mix it with a small amount of acrylic glazing liquid. Paint this over the first color, and then dab the wet paint with the edge of a torn paper towel. This leaves spots of dark color over the lighter color, which looks quite realistic.

Dark-Colored Eyes (Puppies, Brown-Eyed Bunnies)

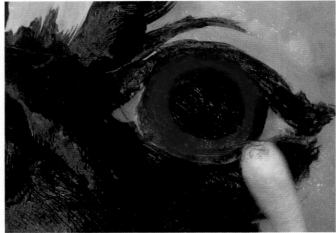

1. Paint the pupil black as shown on the previous page. Also run a dark line around the outside edge of the pupil. When the black is dry, paint the iris reddish brown (Burnt Sienna works well).

2. Mix a dark brown (Burnt Umber) with a bit of glazing liquid. Paint it over the iris, and then remove a bit from the lower corner with a cotton swab. The lighter area should be opposite of the highlight (shown below).

Adding Reflected Light -

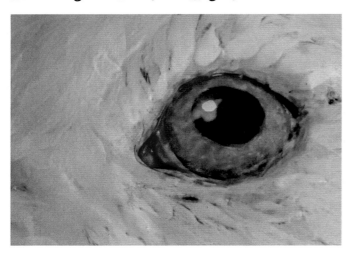

1. When the eye is completely dry, use glazing liquid mixed with dark brown (or, for the white rabbit, reddish brown) and paint this mixture over the eye. Remove almost all of it with a damp paper towel, leaving the darker color only in the deeper edge around the eye. This will outline the eye in a way that looks quite natural.

2. When the glazing liquid is dry, mix a small amount of light blue paint, and brush it onto the eye. Use an irregular outline, not a square or circle. Then put a small dot that's even lighter blue, or pure white. When this reflected light is added to the eyes, your doll will seem to come alive.

Head Armatures

This chapter shows you how to make a lightweight, hollow and seamless base for your doll's head. You will sculpt the individual features of your doll over this armature after it's completely dry.

First, let's learn about the tools and materials -

You'll Need:

- Roll of 4" (10 cm) plaster cloth
- Large bowl of cold water
- One child's sock
- Rice, kitty litter or sand
- Measuring cup
- Glass bottle, weighted if necessary
- Scissors

- Rubber band
- String, dental floss or yarn
- Plastic Tape
- Small plastic bag
- Empty toilet paper roll
- Home-made air-dry clay, see page 8

4" Plaster cloth -

You can find plaster cloth at your local hobby store, or buy it online. I like medical-grade plaster cloth because it dries fast and it's easy to get a nice smooth surface, but hobby store plaster cloth will work, too, and it's easier to find. One roll will give you enough plaster cloth for many doll heads.

Store your plaster cloth in a plastic bag to protect it from moisture in the air.

Large bowl or bucket of water -

Use cold water in a large bowl or bucket, and use new water for every doll head. You don't want plaster to clog up your plumbing, so never pour this water into your sink. Pour it outside, instead.

Your hands will get plaster on them, too, so rinse them off in the bowl instead of the sink.

Child's sock -

The sock is used as a temporary form. I used a Girl's size Small. You can use the same sock over and over again to make as many dolls as you want, but it's nice to have a few extras in case your first one gets a hole in it.

1/4-cup (60 ml), 1/3-cup (80 ml) and a tablespoon (15 ml) -

To measure the...

Rice, kitty litter, or sand -

You can use anything you have on hand to put inside the sock and give it shape, as long as it's easy to pour back out again. I used wheat seeds, because that was what I had in my cupboard. The amount needed for each type of baby animal is shown in the specific instructions that follow.

Glass Bottle -

Your bottle will hold your head armature while you work on the plaster cloth. You can also use your bottle to hold up the heads while you're sculpting the faces and painting them.

The size of your bottle's neck will affect the size of your doll's neck. The neck on the bottle I use has an outside diameter just a tiny fraction over 1" (2.5 cm). This appears to be a fairly standard size, and it works well.

If your bottle is not heavy on the bottom, like mine is, it may tip over when you put the head armature on top. In that case, pour some sand or rice in the bottle to weigh it down.

You'll Also Need:

Plastic tape, dental floss or yarn, and a rubber band -

These will be used to keep the rice inside the sock while you work, and to keep the rice-filled sock firmly attached to the top of the bottle.

Scissors -

Use a pair of scissors with a sharp point, so you can nip just the yarn or floss without cutting a hole in the sock. You can then use the sock to make another doll head. A seam ripper would also work, if you have one.

Empty toilet paper roll (or funnel) and a small plastic bag

The best bags for this project are fold-top sandwich bags. Or use plastic wrap, instead. The TP roll is used as a funnel so the rice goes in the sock instead of all over your floor. If you have an actual funnel, use it instead.

Bunny Head Armatures -

Please be sure to read through this section even if you intend to make a kitten or puppy doll. These instructions will give you a good introduction to the easy process of making your head armatures.

Step 1 - Preparing the Sock

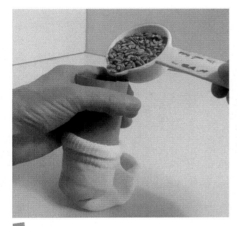

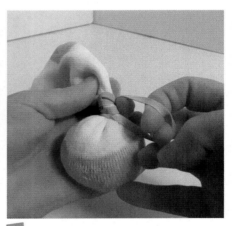

1. Use the TP roll to create a funnel, (or use a real funnel) and pour 1/4 cup (60 ml) of rice or kitty litter into your sock.

2. Push the rice (or whatever you're using) down into the bottom of the sock.

3. Place a rubber band around the sock temporarily, to make it easier to pack the rice in tight.

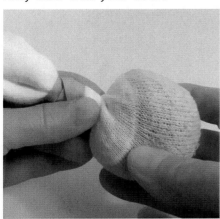

4. Continue to pack the rice down in the sock by twisting the sock above the rubber band.

5. Use your string, yarn or dental floss to tie the "neck" tightly. Remove the rubber band.

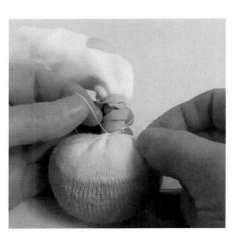

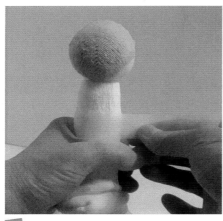

6. Pull the sock down over the neck of the bottle. Put tape tightly around the lower end of the sock, as shown, or use your rubber band.

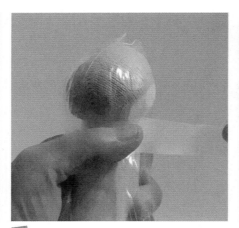

7. Pull the small plastic bag down over the head, and firmly tape around the neck. Use two pieces of tape if needed to take up all the slack in the plastic.

8. Put a small piece of tape over the point where the corner of the bag sticks up.

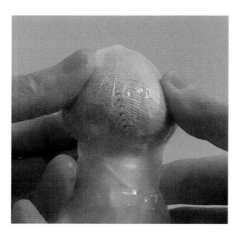

9. Shape the head by pressing on the rice-filled sock. Bunnies have somewhat egg-shaped heads that are rounded in back and pointy in front. The face is narrower at the top and wider on the bottom.

Step 2: Adding the Plaster Cloth

Be sure to keep the plaster cloth and water on opposite sides of your table. You don't want the plaster cloth to get wet by accident. If it does get wet, it must be used quickly.

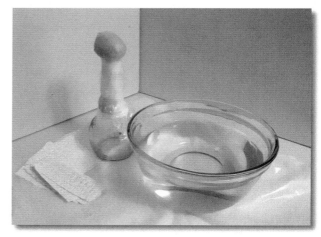

1. Cut four square pieces of plaster cloth 4″ (10 cm) on each side.
Cut two pieces 2″ by 6″ (5 cm x 15 cm) for the ridge around the bottom of the neck.
Cut two pieces 2″ x 4″ (5 cm x 10 cm), for the cheeks.

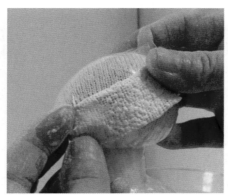

2. Fold a cheek strip into a narrow band and dip it into the cold water for a second.

3. Place the wet strip on the side of the head, slanting up towards the back as shown. Hold it in place for a few seconds to keep it from sliding off the plastic. Then do the second cheek.

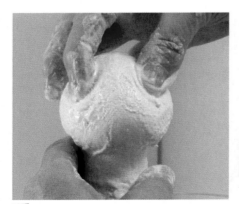

4. Dip one of your big pieces of plaster cloth in the water for a second and drape it over the side of your sock head. Working quickly, pull the cloth around the head and neck, and then rub with your fingers to smooth the plaster over the cloth.

5. Use the other three square pieces to cover the back, the second side, and then the front.

6. Lightly press the head together above the cheeks where the eyes will go.

7. Roll the narrow strips lengthwise and put them around the neck about 1/2" (1.3 cm) from the bottom of the chin. The head should now look like the one shown above. Set it aside to harden.

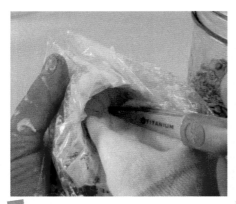

8. The plaster will heat up. When it cools back down, take the head off the bottle and carefully cut the string.

9. Pour the rice back into its container.

10. Pull out the sock, and then pull out the plastic bag. You should be able to use the sock again for another doll..

11. Use a sharp craft knife to cut the ragged edges off the bottom of the neck, and to remove any bumps that may stick out too much.

You can now add your first layer of clay, and both the clay and the plaster will finish drying together.

Step 3: The First Layer of Air-Dry Clay

You'll Need:

- Your new plaster cloth armature
- A batch of home-made air dry clay (see page 8)

This first layer of clay will make your doll head stronger, and it will smooth out the bumps and textures left by the plaster cloth. If the plaster form didn't come out quite symmetrical, you can make minor adjustments to the shape with this first layer—for instance, by making the clay a bit thicker in a spot where the head doesn't seem quite round enough.

1. Put a small piece of clay onto the head. Press the clay with your fingers to stretch and push it up and around the head.

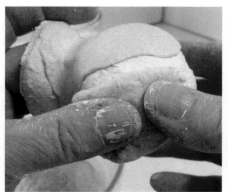

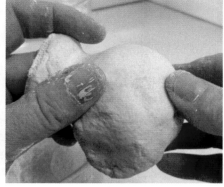

2. Try to spread the clay thinly, but don't make it so thin that you end up with bare spots where plaster shows through.

3. Add additional clay when needed. Smoosh the edges of the new clay into the first piece of clay to firmly attach the two pieces together. You should not be able to see a seam or line where the two pieces come together.

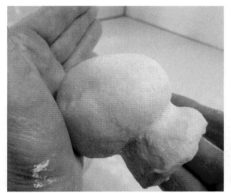

4. Use the palm of your hand to pat the clay smooth, all around. Your head should now have a very thin, even layer of clay that completely covers the plaster, and there should still be a distinct valley between the head and the bottom of the neck. Your clay-covered form should now look like the one shown above.

5. Put the head in front of a fan or in a warm place to dry overnight. Then go to the chapter on sculpting your bunny's head, beginning on page 31.

Kitten Head Armatures —

The kitten's armature is made just like the bunny's, but the shape of the rice-filled sock is much rounder, and you'll add a bit of plaster cloth padding to the muzzle instead of the cheeks.

Use 1/3 cup (80 ml) of rice in your sock. Pat the sock to move the rice around inside until it's quite round, like a ball.

 1. Cut five pieces of plaster cloth, each 4" (10 cm) square.
Cut two pieces 2" x 6" (5 cm x 15 cm) for the neck band.

2. Fold a square piece of plaster cloth about 1" (2.5 cm) on each side. Get it wet and press it to the front of the sock.

3. Cover the muzzle piece and the front of the head with a square piece of plaster cloth. Cover the sides and back with the remaining square pieces, and add the two neck strips, as for the bunny armature (see page 23).

4. Allow the plaster to harden. Then cover with a thin layer of air-dry clay, (not shown, see page 24). Allow to dry overnight before sculpting the features.

Puppy Head Armatures –

There are two different ways to make the open-mouthed muzzle on the puppy armatures. Try it both ways, and see which one you prefer.

Use 1/3 cup (80 ml) of rice, and shape the rice-filled sock as for the bunny, page 22.

If you use the soft-sculpting method to form the muzzle, you will also need some strong thread and a doll needle.

1. Cut four square pieces of plaster cloth, 4" (10 cm) on each side. (If using method #2, you will need five square pieces of plaster cloth.)

Cut two pieces 2" x 6" (5 cm x 15 cm) for the neck band.

Shaping the Muzzle, Method #1:

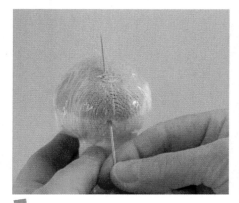

2. Tie a large knot in your thread and put your needle through the plastic bag and sock, as shown,

3. Bring the needle back down again, and then back up, Now pull tightly, to create a dimple for the mouth.

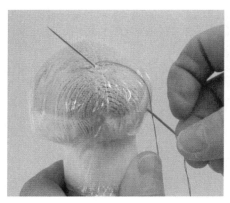

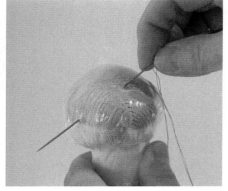

4. Make large stitches on each side of the muzzle and pull tightly, to make a distinct dip between the main part of the head and the muzzle. Make several stitches in the same place, if needed.

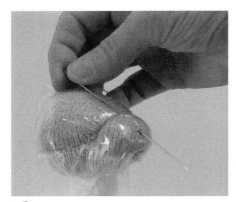

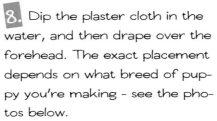

5. Bring the needle from the top of the muzzle to the area where the bottom of the nose will be.

6. Sew a stitch or two going from the bottom of the nose to the mouth, and draw tight. From the side, your sock will now look like the one shown above.

7. Roll one of the square pieces of plaster cloth, corner to corner, as shown.

8. Dip the plaster cloth in the water, and then drape over the forehead. The exact placement depends on what breed of puppy you're making - see the photos below.

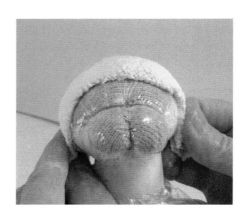

The placement of the forehead determines the length of the muzzle:

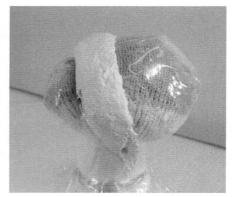

Puppies with standard-sized muzzles, like Retrievers, Shepherds and Pit Bull Terriers.

Puppies with shortened muzzles, like pugs and English bulldogs.

Toy-breed puppies, like Chihuahuas and Pekinese.

  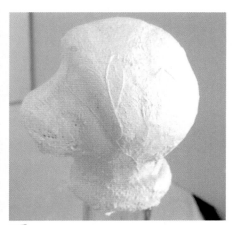

9. Use three square pieces of plaster cloth to cover the two sides and the back.

10. With the last square piece, drape the cloth over the top of the head, and then fold the bottom into a mouth, as shown. This creates a "shelf" for the tongue. Smooth the plaster over the head, and then add the two long strips around the bottom of the neck, as for the bunny, page 23.

Shaping the Muzzle, Method #2:

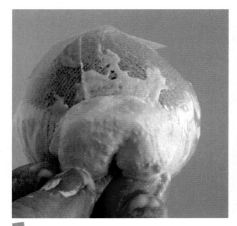  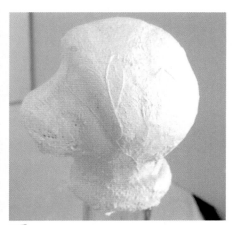

1. Dip one of the four-inch square pieces of plaster cloth in water, and shape it into an inverted "U," as shown above. Place it at the front of the head and hold it for a few seconds to let the plaster stiffens up a bit.

2. Dip a second square piece of plaster cloth in the water, and drape it over the front of the head. Shape the mouth as shown in Step #10, above.

This is a bit tricky, because the first "U" shaped plaster may try to slide off while you're trying to cover it with the second piece.

3. Add the forehead strip now, as shown in the previous instructions starting on #7, page 28. Then cover the side, back and the other side of the head with the remaining square pieces of plaster cloth, and add the neck strips at the bottom. Your armature should now look like the one here, and like the one in step 10, above.

Adding the First Layer of Clay

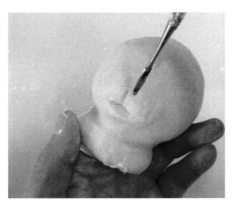

When the plaster has hardened and the rice has been removed, add a thin layer of clay to the plaster cloth head. Follow the instructions for the Bunny, page 25, but when you add clay to the muzzle, use a tool to make sure the mouth does not fill in with clay (unless, of course, you would like your puppy to have a closed mouth). Then make a short mark with your tool from the mouth to the place where the nose will go. Round off the edges of the muzzle on both sides of this line.

Set the head in a warm place or in front of a fan, and allow it to dry overnight.

Baby Bunnies

Lop-eared bunnies come in an amazing variety of sizes and color patterns. They come in almost exactly the same colors and patterns as cats. There are even bunnies with "points" like Siamese cats, and "calico" bunnies with colorful red, gray and black spots.

I picked three common bunny colors that I thought it would be fun to paint, but don't limit yourself to these three colors or patterns. Just remember the only rule for painting baby animal doll heads: pick out your body fabric first!

When your doll is finished, you can dress him or her in some new clothes, using the instructions beginning on page 73 and the patterns beginning on page 89.

Step 1 - Sculpting the Face

You'll Need:

- One head armature (see [age 21)
- One batch of air-dry clay (page 8)
- Small jar of glue mixed with water (page 11)
- Knife or modeling tool
- Soft brush

This is the step that gives your doll his or her unique character. It's fun to see how a small change to a feature can make a big difference in your bunny's personality.

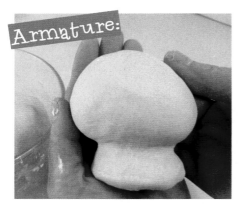

Armature:

Make a bunny head armature using the instructions in the previous chapter.

If your armature didn't come out exactly symmetrical, (mine never do) you can fix it when you add your first layer of clay (see page 24) or when you add the features.

Add the first thin layer of air-dry clay, and allow the armature to dry completely before moving to the next step.

Remember to allow each feature to firm up before adding the next one, so you don't mess up your hard work.

Eyes #1:

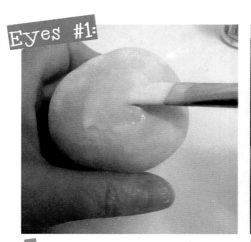

1. Brush your glue mixture just above the middle of the cheek.

2. Roll a small ball of clay with dry fingers, and place it over the glue.

3. Still using dry fingers or thumb, gently tap the balls to make them nice and round.

Nose:

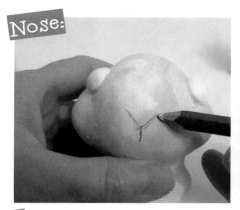  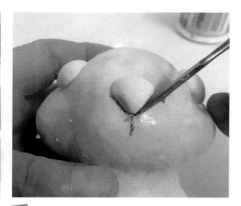

1. Draw three short lines on the front, as shown.

2. Brush the area with glue mix, and then add a small ball of clay to the nose area.

3. Use your modeling tool to give the bottom of the nose its triangular shape.

Muzzle:

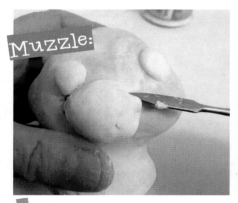 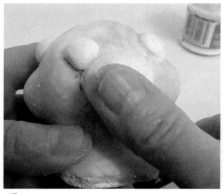 

1. Brush your glue mixture in the muzzle area, and add a small round bit of clay.

2. Use your dry thumb or fingers to shape the clay. (See photo #2 below).

3. Press the edges of the nose and muzzle into the dried head, using your tool and glue mix.

Eyebrows:

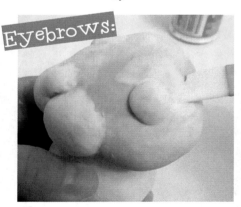 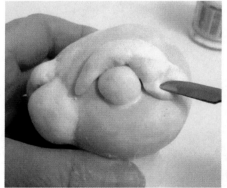 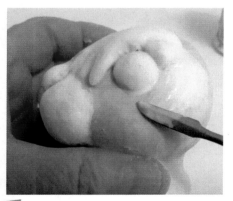

1. When the eye is dry enough to work around safely, brush glue mix above the eye.

2. Press on a noodle of clay, thin at the front and wider at the back. Press into it behind the eye, as shown.

3. Press the excess clay at the back of the eyebrow down around the eye.

Top of Head:

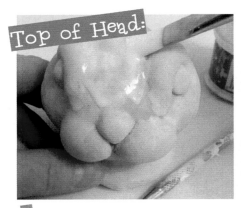 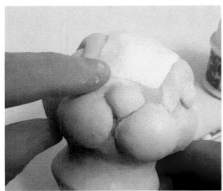 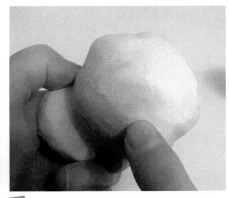

1. Brush glue mix between the eyebrows and add a thin flat piece of clay to the top of the head to fill in between the eyebrows, as shown. Firmly attach the edges with your modeling tool.

2. Use the glue mixture and your finger to smooth the new clay at the back.

Eyes #2

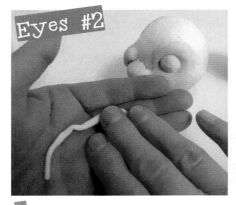 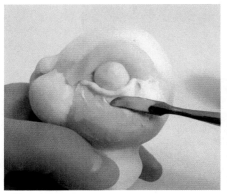 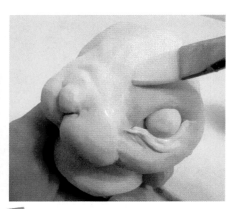

1. Roll out a very thin noodle of clay, Brush glue mix below the eye.

2. Put the noodle in place, and use your tool to attach it firmly to the cheek and behind the eye, while also shaping the lower eyelid as shown in the photo above,.

Finishing:

 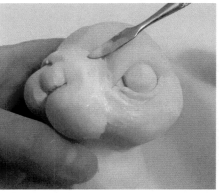 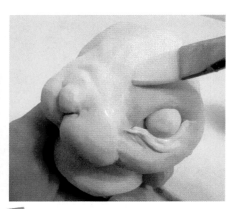

1. Brush on glue mix and add a flat noodle above the nose to define the top of the muzzle.

2. Smooth the edges, and use your tool to create a dip above the nose, as shown.

3. Use your fingers or brush to blend the clay into the forehead.

34

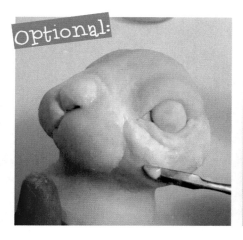

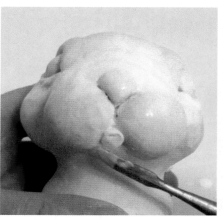

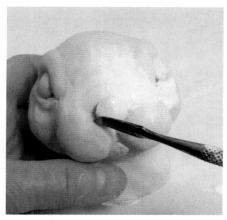

Add a small amount of clay behind the muzzle and below the eye, as shown.

Add a lower lip. (Sometimes I do, and sometimes I don't – see photos on page 31).

Make last-minute changes and repairs. Be sure to brush on glue mix if you add more clay.

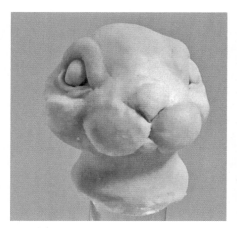

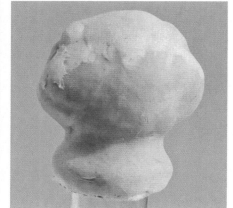

Allow the head to dry completely before moving to the next step.

Step 2 - Cutting Holes for the Ears

You'll Need:

- Your bunny's head, bone dry
- Craft knife with new, sharp blade
- Piece cut from toilet paper tube 1-1/2" (3.8cm) long
- Emery board or strip of sandpaper.

1. Cut a strip from your cardboard tube to measure the curved line you draw on the bunny's head, The ear hole should be 1 ½ inches long. The holes are approximately ½ inch apart at the top of the head, and curve around the back of the eyes.

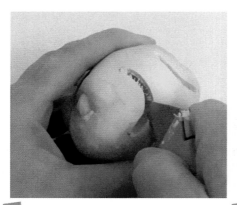
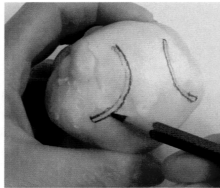
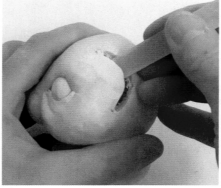
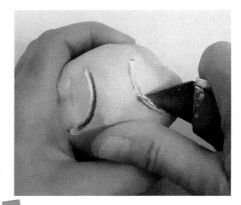

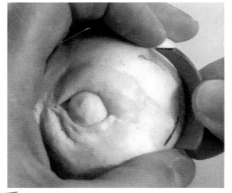

2. Draw two C-shaped lines on the back of the head. Measure the length with the cardboard strip cut from the TP roll.

3. Draw two more lines 1/16" (.16cm) from the first lines, to use as cutting guides.

4. Use your very sharp craft knife to slowly remove material between the lines, one layer at a time.

5. Carefully whittle more material a little at a time, until the hole is 1/8" (.32cm) wide.

6. Smooth the edges with your emery board or sandpaper.

7. Use the cardboard strip to make sure the hole is long enough. Cut more if needed.

Step 3 - Painting the Head

You'll Need:

- Bunny head with ear holes
- Acrylic gesso
- Acrylic paint
- Acrylic glazing liquid (see page 15)

- Cotton swab or paper towels
- Soft brushes
- Matte acrylic varnish
- Clear fingernail polish (optional)

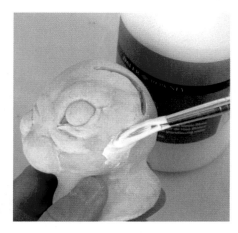

1. Seal the head with a coat of acrylic gesso. Use a soft brush to minimize brush marks. You will probably need two or more layers of gesso to give yourself a nice even coat. The gesso will make your paint colors show up much brighter. Allow the gesso to dry completely before moving to the next step..

2. Add a base coat of the lightest color - for all three bunnies, the base coat was made with Titanium White and a tiny dab of Yellow Oxide (Yellow Ochre). This base coat was allowed to dry.

3. Mix a small amount of red with your white paint, and mix this light pink with Acrylic Glazing Liquid. Brush this mixture over the nose and mouth area, and around the eye. Remove almost all of the pink with a cotton swab or damp paper towel. Allow to dry.

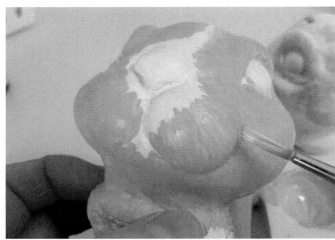

4. Paint spots on the bunnies. I matched my spots to the "camel" velour for the bunny with yellow spots (Yellow Ochre, Titanium White, Burnt Sienna and Burnt Umber). I used the same color as the base coat for the spots on the gray-spotted bunny, but light gray would also work well.

5. Add fur, as described on page 16. Add as many layers of fur as you need to get an interesting mixture of colors. Here, I'm using a dry brush to get very fine lines of lighter fur over the darker yellow. For the gray bunny, use a variety of light and dark gray mixtures, as seen on the photo on the next page.

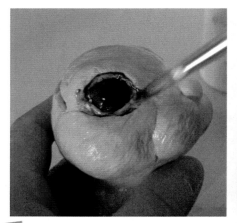

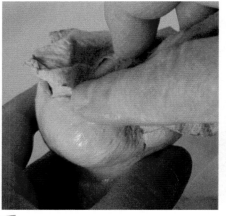

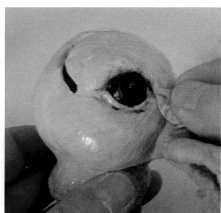

6. For the dark-eyed bunnies, paint the eyes as shown on page 17. Use reddish brown for the first coat, and dark brown (Burnt Umber) for the second coat. When the eyes are dry, mix Burnt Umber (and maybe just a touch of black) with Glazing Liquid. Brush over the eye.

7. Rub off all excess glaze, leaving an outline around the eye, Do the same with the nose. I also used this mix as my last layer of "fur" on the yellow bunny, using a small brush. You'll be able to see how this looked in the next photo, on page 39.

38

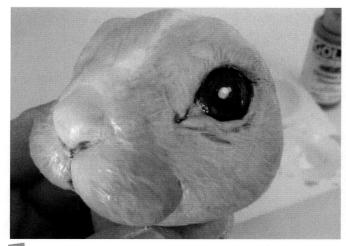

8. When the glaze is dry, add the reflected light to the eye, as described on page 18. When all of the paint is dry, add a coat of matte or satin Acrylic Varnish.

9. When the varnish is dry, you can give the eyes a coat of clear nail polish to make them look shiny and wet.

White Bunny-

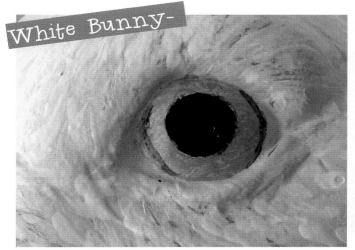

1. This is a blue-eyed white lop-eared bunny. (Some white bunnies have dark pink eyes, and some of them have light brown eyes.) The fur has layers of warm white over layers of cool white (very light gray) to make the all-white fur seem more interesting.

The eyes are painted like the light-colored eyes on page 17, with light blue (Cerulean Blue and White) for the first layer.

2. The second layer of color is a darker blue, made with Ultramarine Blue mixed with Cerulean Blue. This was dabbed off with the torn edge of a paper towel to leave random spots.

3. To finish the eyes and nose area, mix reddish brown (Burnt Sienna) with Acrylic Glazing Liquid, and brush over the eyes and nose. Remove most of the glaze, leaving just enough color to outline the eyes, nose and mouth.

4. Add the reflected light. When all of the paint is dry, add a coat of matte or satin Acrylic Varnish.

5. When the varnish is dry, you can give the eyes a coat nail polish to make them look shiny and wet.

Putting Your Bunny Together

Follow the instructions in the chapter on Bodies (beginning on page 61) to sew the body, arms and ears for your bunny, using a fabric that matches your doll's head. That chapter also shows you how to attach the ears and assemble the doll, and a pom pom tail. Then choose a dress or playsuit from the Clothes chapter, beginning on page 73. You can see the velour colors and dress fabrics and patterns that I chose for my bunnies on the following page.

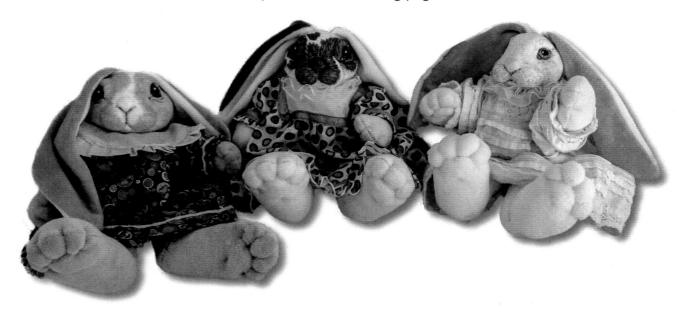

Light Brown Bunny -

The body and ears are made from cotton velour from weirdollsandcrafts.com. The body color is Camel and the velour on the inside of the ears is Cream.

The dress fabric and ribbon was purchased at the local Walmart, and made using the instructions on page 76.

Bunny with Gray Spots -

The body and the inside of the ears are made with Cream velour, and the outside of the ears are Charcoal.

The printed dress fabric is called "Dottie," and was designed by Sharon Turner. The fabric is available at SpoonFlower.com (under the nickname "Scrummy". The instructions for this dress are on page 79. The ribbon is from Walmart.

Blue-Eyed White Bunny -

The body color is Cream, and the insides of the ears are done in Dusty Pink.

The dress was made using the same pattern as the one on the gray spotted bunny, but I used recycled fabric from a child's skirt that I found at the local thrift store. The ribbon around the neck is from a baby's fancy sock.

Kittens

These sweet little kittens are such a joy to make - and there are so many breeds to choose from, you could make lots of them without ever making two alike.

Before starting to make your kitten doll, be sure to read through the more detailed instructions in the Bunny chapter.

Step 1 - Sculpting the Face

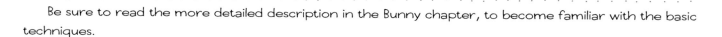

You'll Need:

- One head armature (see page 26)
- One batch of air-dry clay (page 8)
- Small jar of glue mixed with water (page 11)
- Knife or modeling tool
- Soft brush

Be sure to read the more detailed description in the Bunny chapter, to become familiar with the basic techniques.

1. Add the first thin layer of air-dry clay to your kitten's head armature, and allow the armature to dry completely before moving to the next step.

1. Draw your kittens main features on the clay with a soft pencil. (If you put something in the wrong place, or just want to change the size or shape, use a soft eraser to remove the marks and start over.)

2. Paint a small amount of glue and water mixture over the muzzle and eyes. Roll small balls of clay with dry fingers, and place them over the glue, as shown above Pat the wet clay with dry fingers or the palm of your hand to smooth them.

3. Allow the eyes and muzzle to firm up and then paint glue and water mixture around the eyes and on the spot where the nose will go. Add two large noodles of clay for the upper eyelids, and two thinner noodles for the lower eyelids. Add a triangle of clay for the nose, and use a pencil or sculpting tool to create the nostrils.

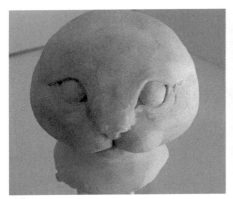

If you're making a portrait doll of a kitten you know, look at a photo or the real kitten to see how much clay to add for the ruff.

If you look at the three kitten heads on the previous page, you see that they're all different. The basic shape of the heads are all the same, but the size and placement of the ruff changes their face, and even affects the "personality" of the doll.

4. Add additional clay to smooth out the space above and between the eyes. Look at the kitten's face and see if it also needs a bit more clay to round out her cheeks. Allow the clay to firm up before finishing.

5. Add a ruff of fur around the outside of the cheeks.

Step 2 - Cutting Holes for the Ears

When the head is completely dry, cut the holes for the ears (see page 36. For your measuring tool, cut a curved strip from your toilet paper roll 1 1/2" long. Place your ears as shown.

Then give your kitten's head one or more coats of Acrylic Gesso.

Calico Kitten

A base coat is applied over the gesso. All three kittens shown here have a base coat made from Titanium White mixed with a tiny amount of Yellow Ocher.

When this warm white was dry, the color patterns were added.

The calico kitten was given a transparent warm brown undercoat for her black spots. When this was dry, light orange was added in the areas that would become red, matching the color to the body velour.

Many coats of fur were added, with lighter and darker versions of the spot colors.

Final details were added by dry-brushing warm white paint from the white areas over the darker spots, and a few random hairs of white and black were painted over the red spots.

The nose was painted with a very light pink, and spots of pink were added in the corners of the eyes, and the mouth,

The eyes were painted as shown on page 17, using a light yellow for the first coat, and light orange for the second coat.

A final glaze was added over the eyes and nose area, made with Burnt Umber and Acrylic Glazing Liquid. The glaze was wiped off, leaving dark brown outlines around the eyes and nostrils.

The reflected light was painted onto the eye, and when all the paint was dry the head was given a protective coat of Acrylic Varnish.

When the varnish was dry, the eyes were given a coat of clear nail polish, to make them shine.

Ragdoll Kitten

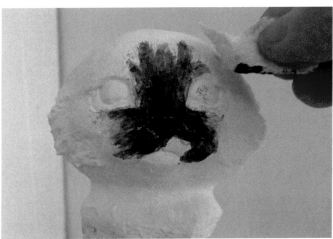

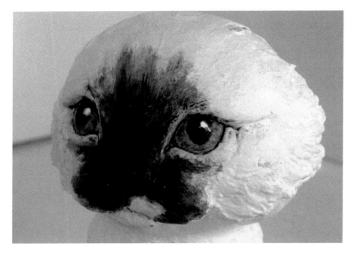

A base coat was applied over the gesso, as for the calico kitten on the previous page. When the warm white base coat was dry, brown paint (Burnt Umber) was mixed with water to make it transparent. This was brushed over the dark areas on the kitten's face.

When the first coat was dry, Burnt Umber was mixed with Black, and this mixture was added to some Acrylic Glazing Liquid. The resulting very dark brown paint was brushed over the dark areas on the kitten's face. To make a smooth transition from the dark areas in the middle of the face to the lighter areas towards the edges, the brown paint was rubbed with a piece of paper towel.

When this second coat was dry, the eyes were painted, as shown on page 17, using Cerulean Blue for the first coat and a mixture of Ultramarine Blue and Cerulean Blue for the second coat. The second coat was dabbed with the edge of a torn paper towel to make realistic color spots in the eyes.

When the eyes were dry, a mixture of Burnt Umber and Acrylic Glazing Liquid was brushed over the eyes and nose area, and most of it was wiped off, leaving a dark line around the eyes, nose and mouth. This glaze was also brushed over the dark area of the face to darken it a bit more and smooth out the brush marks.

The reflected light was painted onto the eye, and when all the paint was dry the head was given a protective coat of Acrylic Varnish.

When the varnish was dry, the eyes were given a coat of clear nail polish, to make them shine.

Orange Tabby Kitten

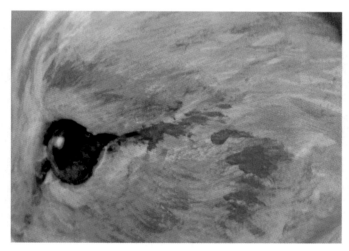

After the base coat of warm white was dry, I painted light yellow over all the areas that would not remain white. When the yellow was dry, I mixed an orange to match the body velour. (Cadmium Red and Cadmium Yellow).

The orange was brushed onto the head in stripes. Where the stripes are lighter, the orange was applied with a dry brush.

Additional coats of fur were added, using slightly lighter and darker colors of yellow and orange. White was also brushed on sparingly, to help give definition to the stripes.

The nose was painted pink, and the eyes were painted as shown on page 17. The base coat on the eyes was light green, and the second coat was dark green. The dark green was dabbed with the torn edge of a paper towel to give a variegated spottiness to the color.

When the green was dry, the spot of reflected light was added, as shown on page 18.

As with the other kittens, a dark brown glaze was brushed on over the eye and nose areas, and then wiped off. When the glaze was dry, the head was given a protective coat of Acrylic Varnish, and the eyes were given a coat of clear fingernail polish.

Putting Your Kitten Together

Follow the instructions in the chapter on Bodies (beginning on page 61) to sew the body, arms and ears for your kitten using a fabric that matches your doll's head. That chapter also shows you how to attach the ears and assemble the doll, and add the kitten's tail. Then choose a dress or playsuit from the Clothes chapter, beginning on page 73. You can see the velour colors and clothes that I chose for my kittens below.

Calico Kitten
The body is made with three different colors: Back, Cream and Rust. one ear is Cream and one ear is Black. As with all the dolls in this book, I purchased the velour from weirdollsandcrafts.com.

The printed dress fabric is called "Tangerine Triangles," and was designed by Sharon Turner (nickname "Scrummy") - available at SpoonFlower.com. The dress was made using the instructions on page 76. The lace and bias tape are from Walmart.

Ragdoll Kitten
The body and ears are made from Cream velour. I used a permanent marker to darken the "points" on the ears.

The lacy T-shirt is made with three baby socks, (instructions on page 73) and the playsuit is made with cotton velour in Jade (instructions on page 74). The buttons were purchased on eBay.

Orange Tabby Kitten
The body and ears are made with tangerine velour.

The T-shirt was made out of an adult sock , and the playsuit fabric was recycled from a man's shirt I purchased at the local thrift store.

Puppies

How could anyone not fall in love with these sweet, huggable puppies?

The puppy dolls are so much fun to make because each one is so different. The expressions and personalities can be changed with slight alterations in the size and shape of the muzzle and eyes. Some puppies have lots of wrinkles, and some puppies have almost no wrinkles at all. And after the sculpting is done, they can be painted in such a wide variety of spots and colors!

I made all of my puppies with their tongues showing in a happy, puppy smile. If you prefer a more sedate look to your puppy doll, you could easily make them with a closed mouth, instead.

Step 1 - Sculpting the Face

The puppies shown here are, from left to right, an English Bulldog, a Chihuahua, a Pug, and a Retriever. Since each breed is so different, I've included separate instructions for each of them.

You'll Need:

- One puppy head armature (see page 27)
- One batch of air-dry clay (page 8)
- Small jar of glue mixed with water (page 11)
- Knife or modeling tool
- Soft brush
- Pencil

| English Bulldog | Chihuahua | Pug | Retriever |

1. Sketch the basic features of your puppy on the armature with your pencil. You may want to look at a photo of a real puppy so you can see how the breed you're making differs from other breeds. For instance, the bulldog and pug armatures have similar muzzle shapes, but the pug has bigger eyes.

Shaping the Cheeks and Muzzle -

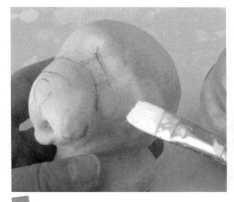

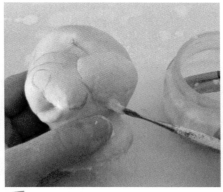

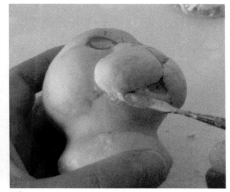

2. Brush the water and glue mixture onto the side of the puppy's head, below the eyes.

3. Add an oval piece of clay to the cheek area.

4. Brush glue mix on the muzzle area and build up the roundness of the muzzle with clay. (See the photos on the following page to see the muzzle shapes of different breeds.)

Adding the Eyes, Nose and Tongue -

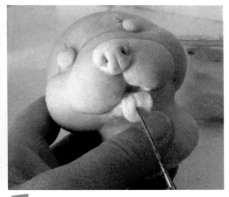

4. Brush the water and glue mixture on the eye, nose and mouth area, Add two small flattened balls for the eyes. Add a nose and a lower lip. Shape the nose as shown above.

5. Create a very flat oval-shaped tongue.

6. Brush glue and water mixture inside the mouth, and carefully insert the back end of the tongue. Use your tool to make sure it's well attached at the back, and to form a line down the middle, as shown.

Adding Eyelids -

7. When the eyes are firm enough to work around without damage, brush glue mix above and below the eye and add a thin noodle of clay to create upper and lower eyelids. Look at the photos on the next page to see how the eyes look on different breeds.

English Bulldog

The bulldog puppy has a round head, and a wide, flat muzzle. There are deep bags below the eyes, and the eyelids cover almost half of the upper portion of the eye. The nose is large.

Chihuahua

The Chihuahua has a delicate little muzzle., bright, open eyes, a very small nose, and thin upper and lower eyelids.

Pug

The pug has a very wide muzzle and round cheeks, and thick upper and lower eyelids. The eyes are wide open. The nose is smaller than the bulldog's, but bigger than the Chihuahua's.

Retriever

The retriever has nice fat cheeks and a fairly narrow muzzle. She has lazy-looking eyes, with upper lids that cover almost half of the eye and lower lids that droop. The nose is fairly large.

Adding Wrinkles and Finishing Up:

By this time, the basic shapes of your puppy's features have been established. Now we add a bit of clay to all of the puppies to finish them. How much to add, and where to add it, depends on the breed. Remember to brush on some glue and water mixture before adding more clay.

English Bulldog

The bulldog puppy has lots and lots of wrinkles. I started with the wrinkles that sit above the eyes, and then added the small noodle of clay just above the nose. Then I added the really big noodle that goes from the top of the head, around behind an eye and around the cheek, over the nose, and up and around the other side. A few more smaller pieces fill in the rest.

Because the wrinkles are such a prominent feature of this breed, you may want to find a good photo of a bulldog puppy, to have as your model as you work.

Chihuahua

Compared to the English Bulldog, there is very little left to do to finish the Chihuahua. She just needs a bit of clay to smooth out the area between the eyes and on the forehead. Take a good look at her head from all directions, and make sure it's nice and round. You may need to add additional clay to the back or sides of the head to get that rounded look.

Pug

The pug has some wrinkles, like the English Bulldog, but they aren't nearly as extreme. The important features are the eyebrows that bend sharply just above the eye, giving the pug its distinctive expression. There is also a fairly large fold over the muzzle between the eyes, and a smaller one just above the nose.

Retriever

The retriever gets more clay to fill in the space between the eyes and above the eyelids, and two small flat balls that create distinct eyebrows. One flat piece of clay over the muzzle finishes the sculpting for this puppy.

With minor variations, this head could be used for Pit Bull Terriers, Australian Shepherds, and any number of the larger breeds. Make the eyes larger and the lower lid droopier, and you'd have a basset hound.

Step 2 - Cutting Holes for the Ears

You'll Need:

- Your puppy's head, bone dry
- Craft knife with new, sharp blade
- Piece cut from toilet paper tube 1-3/4" (3.8 cm) long
- Emery board or strip of sandpaper.

Cut a strip from your cardboard tube to use to help measure the curved line you draw on the puppy's head, as shown for the bunny, page 36,

Almost all breeds have ears that have a similar shape. However, the ears are attached at slightly different places on the head, and they hang, fold, or stand up straight, depending on the type of puppy you're making. For the four breeds in this chapter, cut the ear holes as shown below.

If you're making a different breed than the ones I made, look carefully at photos to find the right placement for the ears. It also helps to cut out a paper pattern of the ears (without the seam allowance, of course) and hold it up to your puppy's head to determine where the ears will look best.

  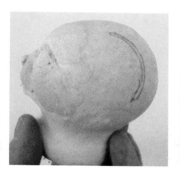 

English Bulldog Chihuahua

Pug Retriever

55

English Bulldog Puppy -

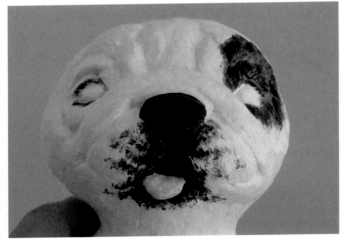

1. A base coat of warm white was painted over the entire head. When it was dry I painted the large spot around one eye, and a bit of "mascara" around the other eye, using a light brown paint (Burnt Sienna). The second coat of fur was a darker brown (Burnt Umber).

2. When the base coat was dry, I painted the nose black, and used black paint to create the dark spots on the muzzle. Then a very dark brown was used as another layer of fur over the brindled markings on the large eye spot. The tongue and eye corners were painted pink.

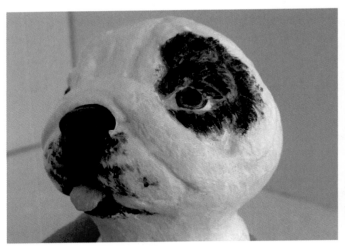

3. The eye was painted, first with reddish brown, and then with dark brown, as shown on page 18. When the eyes were dry, a glaze was brushed on and then wiped off, leaving a line around the eyes and a bit of darker color to help define the deep recesses between the wrinkles.

4. After the eyes were finished and the head was varnished, I added the ears. Two hidden stitches on the inside of each ear keep the ears folded as shown. Bulldogs have many different types of ears - look up photos to find the ear style you like best.

Chihuahua Puppy -

1. Most of the head was painted black, and the muzzle and eyebrows were painted light yellow. (Titanium White, Cadmium Yellow Light, and a touch of Burnt Sienna). Chihuahuas have many different colors and patterns, so look for photos online to find a good model for your doll.

2. Darker yellow was brushed over the light areas, and a bit more was brushed on under the eyes to highlight our Chihuahua's bright, happy expression. The tongue and the corners of the eyes were painted light pink.

3. The eyes were painted, as shown on page 18. When the eyes were dry, dark brown glaze was applied, and then wiped off, leaving just a bit of color around the eyes and the edges of the muzzle.

4. The highlights were added to the eyes, the head was varnished, and the eyes, nose and tongue got their coat of clear fingernail polish.

My Chihuahua has huge ears. One of them stands straight up, and I used my steam iron to create a gentle fold in the other ear.

Pug Puppy -

1. Light brownish yellow was painted over the back of the head, (Titanium White, Yellow Ochre and a smidgen of Burnt Umber). The muzzle and around the eyes was painted dark brown (Burnt Umber mixed with a bit of Black).

2. To make the large color areas a bit more interesting, I brushed on slightly darker tan over the back of the head, and used a very dark brown over the muzzle. The nose was painted black. The tongue and the corners of the eyes are painted light pink.

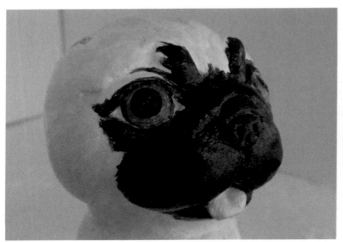

3. The eyes were painted, as shown on page 18. When the eyes were dry, dark brown glaze was brushed over the face, and then wiped off. I allowed the color to remain in the wrinkles, and between the eyes to soften the edges of the dark facial markings (see next photo).

4. The highlights were added to the eyes, the head was varnished, and the eyes, nose and tongue got their coat of clear fingernail polish.

The pug's ears have a hidden stitch to keep them folded down towards the face, I used charcoal velour on the ears, but black would have worked, too.

Golden Retriever Puppy -

1. I started the retriever's main color with very warm white (Titanium White with Yellow Ochre) and built up several layers of fur with progressively darker yellow paint.

2. I added Burnt Sienna and Cadmium Yellow Light to the original light yellow to continue building up the golden fur. The nose and lips were painted black, and the tongue and the corners of the eyes were painted pink.

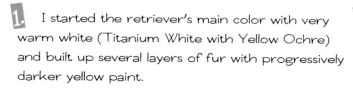

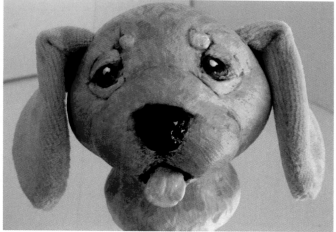

3. The eyes were painted, as shown on page 18. Then dark brown glaze was brushed over the eye area and wiped off, leaving a line around the eyes and color deep in the lines around the eyebrows and eyelids (see next photo).

4. The highlights were added to the eyes, the head was varnished, and the eyes, nose and tongue got their coat of clear fingernail polish.

The retriever's ears have a hidden stitch to keep them folded down and forward towards the face.

Putting Your Puppy Together

Follow the instructions in the chapter on Bodies (beginning on page 61) to sew the body, arms and ears for your puppy, using a fabric that matches your doll's head. Attach the ears and assemble the doll, and add a tail. Then choose a dress or playsuit from the Clothes chapter, beginning on page 73. For a detailed look at the tails, see page 72.

English Bulldog Puppy

The body and ears are made with Cream velour. The T-shirt was made out of three baby socks (instructions on page 73) and the playsuit was made out of a recycled T-shirt (instructions on page 74). All of the buttons on this page were bought on eBay.

Chihuahua Puppy

The body and ears are Black cotton velour. The playsuit was made with Camel velour, and the T-shirt was made out of three baby socks.

Golden Retriever Puppy

The body and ears are Camel velour. The printed dress fabric was designed by Sharon Turner. The design is called "teenie baby star mosaic," and you can find it at Spoonflower.com under the nickname "Scrummy." The ruffle around the collar is 1/2" bias tape, from Walmart.

Pug Puppy

The body is cotton velour in Camel, the ears are Charcoal. The dress fabric was designed by Maudie&Ma. It's called "Jungle Babies," and it's available at Spoonflower.com. The lace and ribbon are from Walmart.

Sewing the Bodies

The soft, huggable bodies and ears are easy to sew and sculpt. In fact, you could do all of the sewing by hand, if you don't have a sewing machine. If you aren't familiar with hand-sewing techniques, or if you'd like to learn more about sewing in general, you should be able to pick up a great book at your local library.

You'll Need:

Cotton Velour -

The bodies for all of the dolls in this book are made with cotton velour. The fabric is slightly stretchy, which allows you to hand-sculpt the toes and ankles with just a few stitches. It's also slightly fuzzy, which makes it feel silky-smooth (and it helps to hide little sewing boo-boos, which is kind of nice, I think).

This fabric is not available at my local fabric shop, but I found a source online that has a great selection of colors, and they ship very fast. You can find them at: weirdollsandcrafts.com

I ordered my doll needles and wool stuffing from them, too. If you live in a larger city, your local fabric store probably caries at least a few colors of velour.

A "fat quarter" of this fabric is 18" x 28" (46 cm x 71 cm). This is enough fabric for two dolls. You may even end up with a few small scraps you can use for contrasting ears or arms on another doll.

You'll find the patterns and cutting charts for each doll in the Body Patterns chapter, beginning on page 81. In the next few pages you'll see how the pieces are sewn together, and how to sculpt those adorable toes.

Stuffing -

You can use either polyester fiberfill or wool stuffing - either type will work just fine. I enjoyed working with the wool stuffing I bought, but the polyester stuffing is available almost everywhere, and it's less expensive.

Don't stuff your dolls too tightly. If you make the stuffing too tight, it will be difficult to sculpt your doll's toes and ankles.

Thread and Dental Floss -

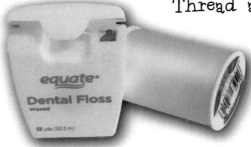

Use regular sewing thread when sewing the body pieces together. For the sculpting, you can use heavy craft thread in a color that matches the fabric, or waxed dental floss. I prefer the floss, because it seems to hold the sculpting stitches a bit tighter—but you can try both and see which one you prefer. The fuzz on the velour will cover the sculpting stitches, but the floss may still show on very dark fabric.

Doll Needles -

Doll needles are used for the sculpting and for attaching the arms. I use 3-½" and 5" needles for my dolls. They are not always stocked in smaller fabric stores, but you can find them online.

Buttons -

I like to use buttons when attaching the arms, but you don't really need them, so they're optional.

Fabric Marking Pen or Chalk -

To trace around the patterns.

A Few Tips for Sewing

Seam allowances -

The seam allowance on the main body part is 1/4" (6 mm). The seam allowance on arms, ears and tails is 1/8" (3 mm). Since you'll sew the smaller pieces before cutting them, this narrow seam allowance isn't as scary as it sounds.

Anchor your thread -

At the beginning of each seam, backstitch once or twice to make sure your seam is anchored in place.

When sculpting with your doll needles, anchor the thread at the beginning with several small stitches, to keep your knot from pulling through the fabric. You will see instructions to anchor the thread at other points in the sculpting process, too.

Keep your scraps -

You can use bits and pieces that are left over to make contrasting ears for another doll.

Step 1 - Sewing

1. Choose the pattern pieces for the doll of your choice (starting on page 81). You will need to connect the two halves of the body pattern, as instructed in the pattern chapter. Trace the pattern from the book and then transfer it onto the wrong side of your velour with a marking pen. (Or use chalk if your velour is very dark). I like to use patterns cut out of poster board, because they can be used over and over again.

Cut out the two body pieces, but don't cut the arms, ears or tail quite yet.

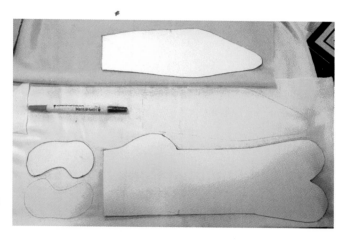

2. Sew the front and back center seams on the body. Clip the seams where the legs begin.

3. Then fold the legs together and sew, beginning each leg seam at the crotch.

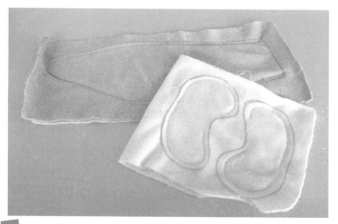

4. With right sides together, sew 1/8 inch (3 mm) inside the marked lines on your ears, tails and arms. Be sure to leave an opening on the arms for turning.

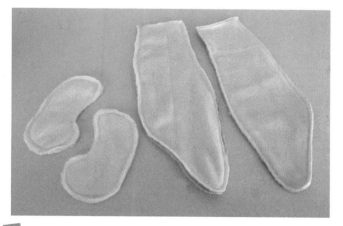

5. Trim the seams on the arm, ear and tail (not shown).

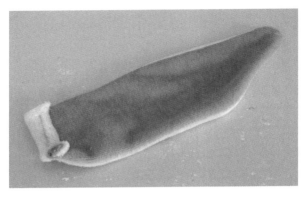

6. Turn all pieces right-side out.

7. Roll up the bottom 1/2" (1.5 cm) at the bottom of the ears, and then roll again. This will create a thick roll of fabric, as shown. The six layers of fabric, plus the materials at the seams, may not fit under the pressure foot on your sewing machine, so just stitch the center portion, or do this by hand. This thick roll of fabric will keep the ear from coming loose after it has been pulled through the ear holes on the head.

Step 2 - Stuffing and Sculpting the Toes

You'll Need:

- Your body and arms, sewn as shown above
- Matching craft thread or waxed dental floss
- Wool or Polyester stuffing
- Doll needle
- Measuring tape

1. Put stuffing in the arms and legs. The stuffing should be well-filled but not too tight. Thread your needle with about 18" of craft thread or dental floss. (In the photos, I'm using a very thick dark thread so you can see the stitches, but I normally use waxed dental floss. I think it's much easier to use. If you do use craft thread, choose a color that matches your velour.

If you'd like to watch over my shoulder as I sculpt the toes, you can find a video at:
UltimatePaperMache.com/dolls

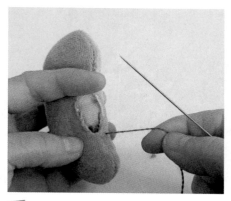 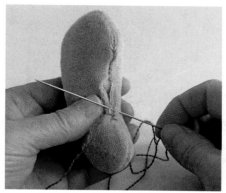 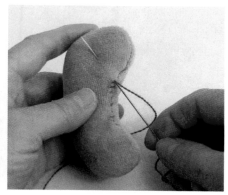

2. Knot the thread or floss and sew the opening in the arms with small overcast stitches, beginning at the narrow end and working toward the paw.

3. Put the point of your needle at the beginning of the first toe, and pull the thread through.

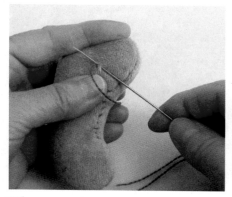 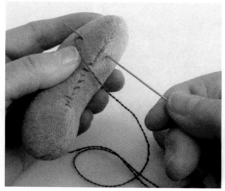 

4. Anchor your thread.

5. Put your needle point just on the other side of the seam, and put it through the fabric and stuffing to the point where it was anchored.

6. Pull this long stitch tight, then make another stitch on top of it, with the needle point coming out at the beginning of the next toe, as shown.

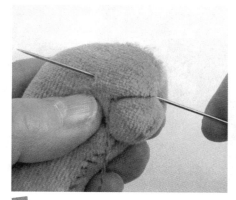 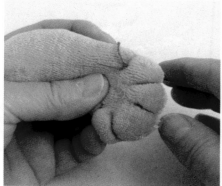 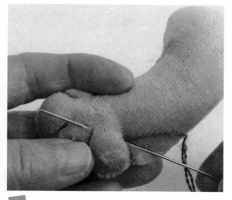

7. Make two tight stitches between each toe, until you have all four toes.

8. Make a tight stitch at the bottom of the end toe, pulling it tight.

9. Begin to sculpt the bottom of the toes by making large, tight stitches, as shown.

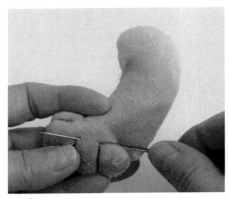

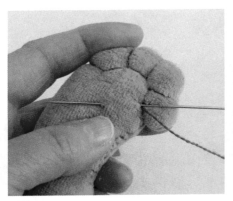

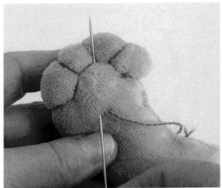

10. Continue until there's a stitch below each toe. Pull each stitch tight to make the toes nice and round.

11. Put the needle tip at the point shown, to begin making a dimple that will define the pad.

12. Take a short stitch at the bottom of the pad, and bring the thread up to a spot where two toes come together,

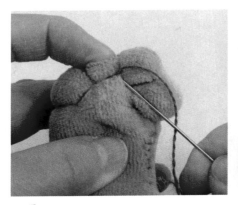

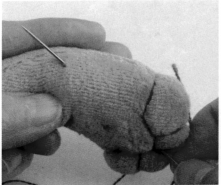

13. Pull the thread to make a dimple at the bottom of the pad. Take several small stitches in one spot, to anchor the thread just below a toe, where it will not be seen, as shown. Then put the needle point a few inches away from the paw, and cut.

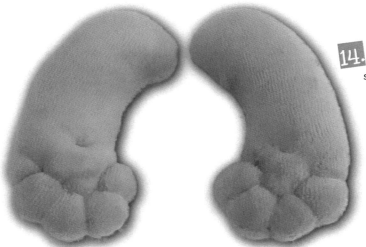

14. Sculpt the paw on the other arm, making sure to put the toes on the opposite side, as shown. This will give you a right and left arm.

Now, give your doll's feet some toes, too, in exactly the same way. When the toes have been sculpted, it will be time to create the heel and ankle, as shown on the next page.

Step 3 - Sculpting the Ankles

The size of your doll's feet are determined by the placement of the heel and ankle. The bunny's feet are much larger than the kitten's and puppies feet.

Begin the heel and ankle on your bunny 3 ½" (9 cm) from the tip of the toes. For the kittens and puppies, the ankle and heel begin 2" (5 cm) from the tip of the toes.

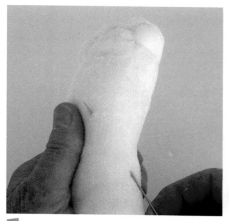

1. Bring a new 18" (46 cm) thread through the stuffing for the heel. See paragraph above for placement.

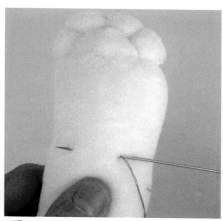

2. Anchor the thread with several small stitches, and then put the needle through the heel, as shown.

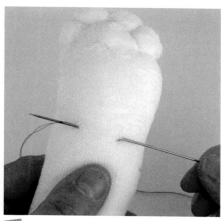

3. Bring the thread around the leg, and put your needle back through the heel.

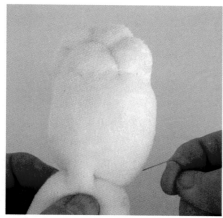

4. Pull the thread very tight.

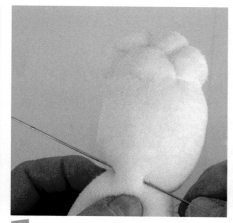

5. Make a second stitch around the leg, to make it nice and secure. Pull tight.

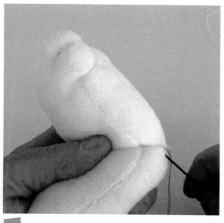

6. Fold the foot forward over the indentation made by your stitch. Hold it tight.

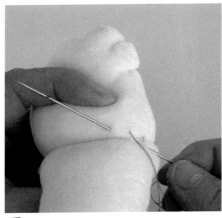

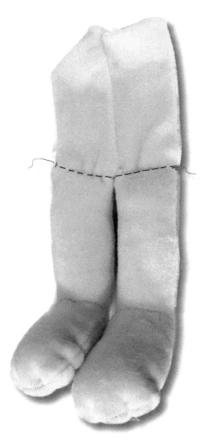

7. Use an overhand stitch to secure the foot in place around the ankle, as shown,

8. Anchor your thread and hide the end, as shown on page 66. Now, do the other foot.

9. Sew across the top of the legs, as shown. (Use matching thread, of course).

. . . .

Gathering the Neck Fabric -

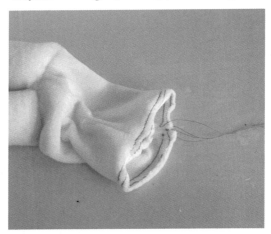

Before stuffing the rest of the body, sew two rows of long basting stitches around the neck. You can do this by hand or with your machine. If using a sewing machine, set it to the longest stitch.

Begin each line of stitching at the center back, about 1/4" (6 mm) from the top edge, and put the lines of stitching 1/8" (3mm) apart. Don't cross the lines of stitching, and don't anchor the end of the row.

Leave a very long tail of thread, so you can easily grasp the free ends to gather the fabric.

Now set the body aside while you attach the ears to the head.

Attaching Ears

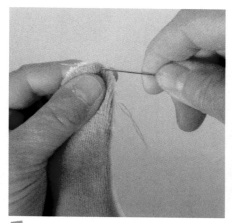

1. With a doll needle, put a large stitch in the seam on the tip of the ear with a double strand of heavy thread.

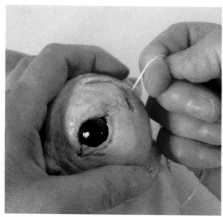

2. Put your needle through the neck and then out the ear hole. Pull gently on the thread to pull the ear up to the ear hole.

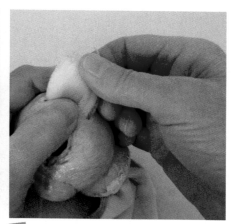

3. As soon as you can reach it, grasp the tip of the ear and work it slowly upward.

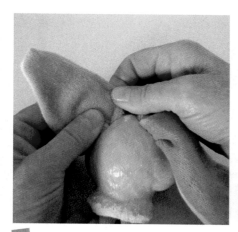

4. Stop and rearrange the fabric if it tries to fold over.

5. When all of the ear has been pulled through, carefully clip off the thread.

Ears for all of the other baby animals are done the same way. The puppy ears will not naturally fold over, like the bunny ears do, so you will need to make small stitches to hold the ears in the right position. This is described in the Puppy chapter for each breed, beginning on page 56.

Attaching the Head

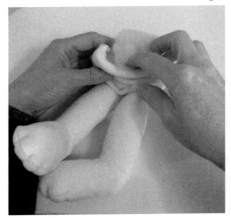

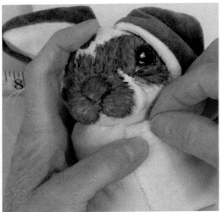

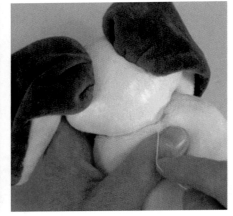

1. Stuff the body, but not too tightly. You need to leave enough room for the neck.

2. Put the head in the body and fold the neck material so the gathering threads (see page 68) are hidden inside.

4. Pull the threads tight. Use your doll needle to anchor the ends so the head is held fast.

You should not be able to see the threads, and the fabric should be evenly spaced around the neck.

Attaching the Arms

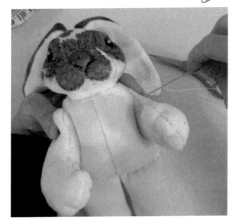

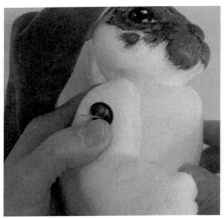

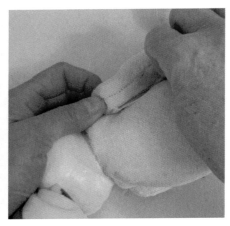

1. Use your longest doll needle and about 18" (46 cm) of heavy thread. Tie a knot in one end, and push the needle through the arms and body, just below the neck.

2. Go back and forth, pulling the thread tight each time. You can also use buttons, if you want, but it isn't absolutely necessary.

3. When you run out of thread, anchor or tie the thread in a hidden spot under an arm.

Adding the Tails

Bunny tails -

1. Choose a soft yarn to make a pom-pom tail. The tail on the left is made from Bernat's Pipsqueak, a polyester yarn with little fluffy threads sticking out its entire length.. The tail on the right is made with cotton yarn.

2. Cut a piece of light cardboard about 3" (8 cm) long and 3/4" (2 cm) wide. Make short slits in the ends, as shown in step 3, below.

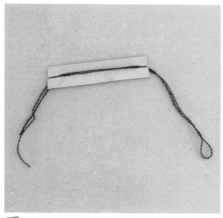

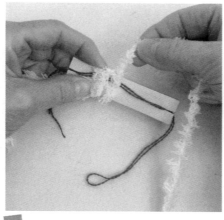

3. Use the slits in the cardboard strip to hold the ends of a 10" (26 cm) piece of yarn, as shown, (but of course you'll want to use the same yarn that you use for your tail.)

4. Wrap a long piece of yarn around the cardboard to make a pom-pom.

5. When it seems full enough, bring the ends of the short yarn up around the pom-pom.

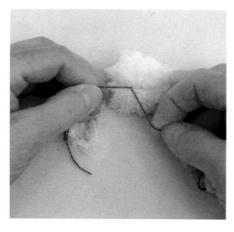

6. Tie the short yarn tightly (a second pair of hands really helps for this step).

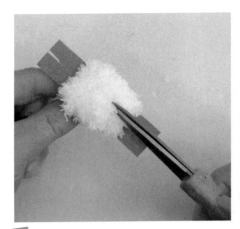

7. Turn the cardboard over and cut through the middle of the yarn on the other side.

8. When the cardboard has been removed, fluff out the pom-pom, and trim it to make a round fuzzy ball.

9. Use heavy craft thread or waxed dental floss to attach the tail to your bunny's rear end.

Kitten and puppy tails -

Choose the tail pattern for the doll of your choice, (page 83). Sew the tail the same way as the arms, shown on page 63. Then add stuffing to the tail. You may need to use a small dowel or the eraser-end of a pencil to get the stuffing all the way into the tip of the tail. Sew the tails onto the doll's rear end with heavy craft thread.

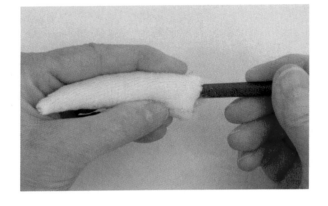

The kitten and Chihuahua tails will look like the retriever tail shown below, on the left. The bulldog puppy's tail is quite short, and the pug's tail is twisted into a corkscrew and held in that position with a few hidden stitches.

Sewing the Clothes

Sock T-Shirt

You'll Need:

- One baby sock with tall cuff or crew-style top
- Two more socks, can be any style
- Matching thread

Since the socks are so stretchy, the size doesn't seem to matter — just pick the ones that will look best on your doll.

You might prefer to sew your t-shirt by hand, since using the machine on such small stretchy parts is a bit tricky. If you do use your machine, try to find socks that are tightly knit - if the weave is too loose, the socks will be drawn down inside your sewing machine.

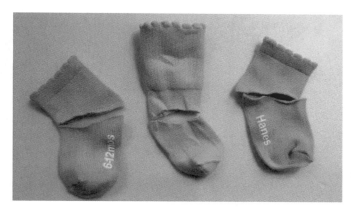

1. Cut the long sock just above the heel, to make the neck and body of the t-shirt. Cut the two short socks through the heel, for the arms. The arms will then have a longer side, which goes at the top to create the shoulder.

2. Measure the cut edge of the arms. Cut two slits in the long sock for the arms, beginning at least ½" (1.25 cm) from the top.

3. Turn the long sock inside out, then place the arms inside and sew the arms to the body, right sides together. Turn up the bottom edge and hem with a zigzag stitch to finish.

73

Playsuit

You'll Need:

- Fat quarter of fabric of your choice
- Matching thread
- Matching or contrasting buttons

You can use cotton velour, a recycled T-shirt, or woven cotton. Stretchy fabrics work really well, and are easy to get on the doll without making buttonholes.

1. Cut out two main pieces and one facing, using the patterns beginning on page 94.

2. Sew the front center seam.

3. Turn under the bottom edge of the facing and hem it, to give a finished edge. (I cut my facing from the bottom edge of a recycled T-shirt, so it was already hemmed).

With right sides together, sew the top of the facing to the top of the main pieces, as shown.

4. With the right sides together and the facing turned up, sew the center back seam. Since your doll has a tail, you need to leave a 2" (5 cm) opening in the seam, starting about 1 ½" (4 cm) from the top of the playsuit. Press the seam open, and then sew around the edges of the tail opening to give it a nice finish.

5. Measure around the lower leg of your doll, and use this measurement to cut two pieces of 1/4" (6 mm) elastic. Turn under 3/4" (2 cm) on the bottom of the playsuit leg. Sew the elastic ½ inch from the bottom of the leg, stretching the elastic as you sew.

6. With right sides together, sew the inseam.

7 Turn the playsuit right-side out, and sew buttons over the ends of the straps and the top corners of the playsuit, as shown. If you used fabric that doesn't stretch enough to get the playsuit on without buttonholes, sew buttonholes in the straps first, using the instructions that came with your machine, and sew the buttons to the top corners of the playsuit. When you put the playsuit on your doll, her tail will stick out, like this:

Dress with Collar

You'll Need:

- Fat quarter of fabric of your choice
- Matching thread
- Lace, ruffle and/or trim of your choice

1. Cut out one dress front, two dress backs, and one collar, using patterns beginning on page 89.

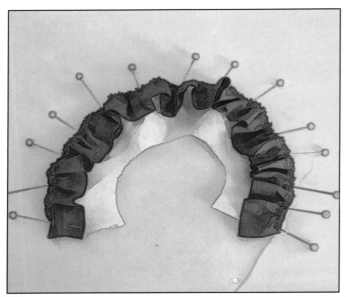

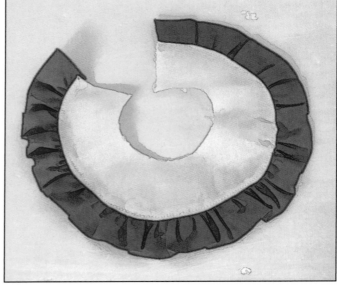

1. Cut a ruffle or lace about twice as long as the outside edge of the round collar. Run a row of long basting stitches down the ruffle or lace and gather to fit the collar. Turn under the back edge of the collar and stitch. Pin the ruffle or lace to the collar, as shown.

2. Stitch the ruffle or lace to the collar. Turn, press, and top stitch. Turn under the back edge and stitch to give it a finished edge.

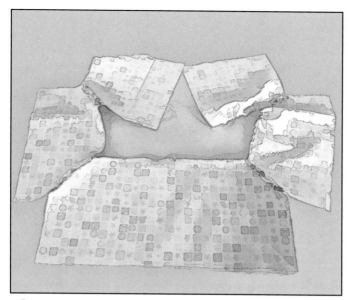

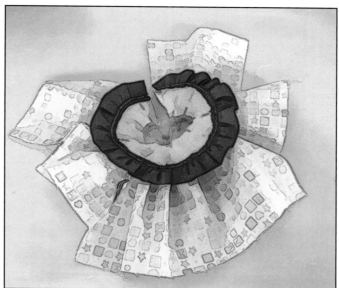

3 With right sides together, sew the raglan sleeves to the front and back pieces, as shown. Run a line of long stitches around the neck edge of the dress, and pull on the thread to gather the top edge to fit the neck edge of the collar.

4. Turn under the top back center edges of the dress fabric ¼" (6 mm). Pin the right side of the collar to the wrong side of the dress. Make sure the gathers are spread evenly, and the center front of the dress is even with the center front of the collar.

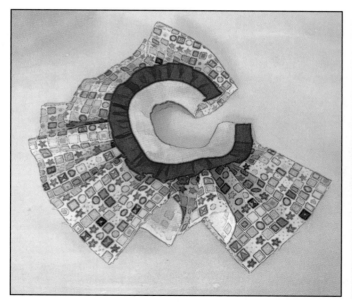

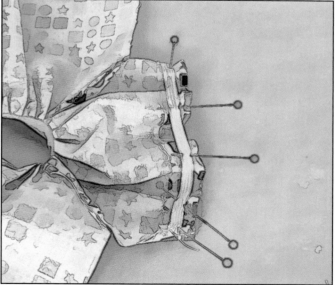

5 Sew the gathered dress to the collar. Clip the curved seam, turn and press.

6. Measure around the doll's arm, and use this measurement to cut a piece of 1/4" (6 mm) elastic. (Or use ribbon, as shown on page 80). Turn under ¾ inch (19 mm) on the sleeves, pin the elastic to the back side of the sleeve and sew.

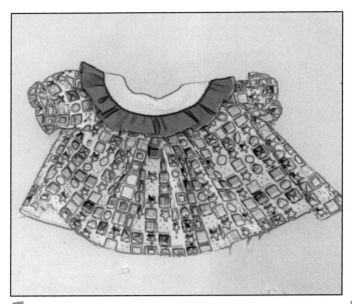

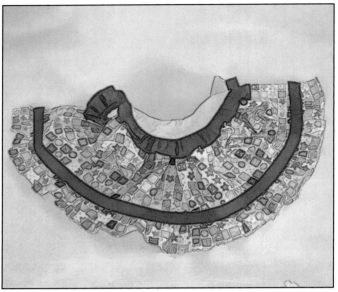

7. With right sides together, sew the side seams.

8. Cut lace or a ruffle twice as long as the bottom edge of the dress. Gather, pin, and sew, right sides together. Turn, press, and top stitch, or add a piece of ribbon, bias tape, or other trim.

9. Sew the back center seam, stopping two inches below the collar. Turn the edges of the opening and press, then stitch.

I use a few small stitches at the top of the neck to hold the dress on the doll, but you may prefer to use a hook and eye.

Dress with Yoke

You'll Need:
- Fat quarter of fabric of your choice
- Matching thread
- Lace, ruffle and/or trim of your choice

1. Cut out one dress front, and two dress backs. The patterns begin on page 89.

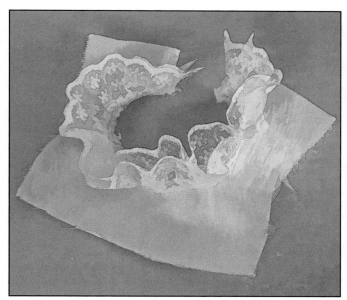

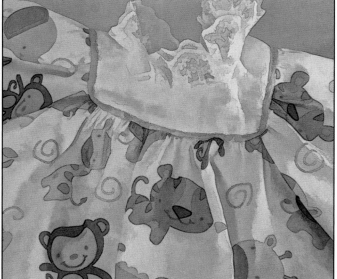

1. Cut a ruffle or lace about twice as long as the neck edge of the square yoke. Run a row of long basting stitches down the ruffle or lace and gather to fit the collar. Turn under the back edge of the yoke and stitch to give it a finished edge. Pin the ruffle or lace to the neck, right sides together, and sew. Turn and top stitch.

I used the top of a baby's lace-topped sock, including about 1/4" (6 mm) of knitted sock fabric.

2. Sew the sleeves, dress front and dress back pieces together, as shown in step 3, page 77. Gather the top edge, Turn under the top back center edges of the dress fabric ¼ inch (6 mm). Pin the gathered dress pieces to the outside edge of the square yoke, right sides together, matching the seams to the yoke corners. Stitch, turn, press and topstitch, or cover the seam with trim, as shown.

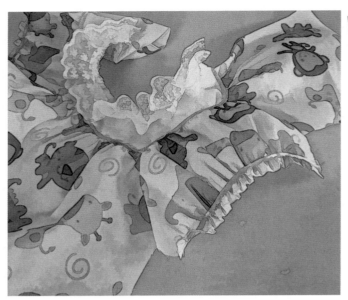

3. To use ribbon instead of elastic around the sleeves, measure the doll's arm and add 3/4". Use this measurement to cut two pieces of ribbon. Turn under ¾ inch on the sleeve, run a row of wide stitches 1/2" (12 mm) from the folded edge, and gather to fit the ribbon. Sew the ribbon on the right side of the sleeve.

Finish the dress as shown on page 78.

Body Patterns

You'll Need:

- Tracing paper
- Pen or pencil
- Poster board or light cardboard (optional)

Choose the pattern pieces that fit the doll of your choice, and trace them onto tracing paper. If you prefer to use a stiffer pattern, just cut out the tracing paper pattern and then trace around that onto poster board or light cardboard.

Use a fabric marking pen or chalk to transfer the pattern onto your fabric.

Joining Large Pattern Pieces

Several patterns were too big to fit onto one page in this book, like the body pattern shown below. Just trace the first half of the pattern, including the dark line that marks the connection of the two pieces, and then move your tracing paper over, so the dark line on the second pattern piece is under the dark line you drew on your tracing paper, The two pieces should now line up, and you'll be able to complete the other side of your pattern. You will probably need to tape two pieces of paper together to make a piece big enough for the joined pattern piece to fit.

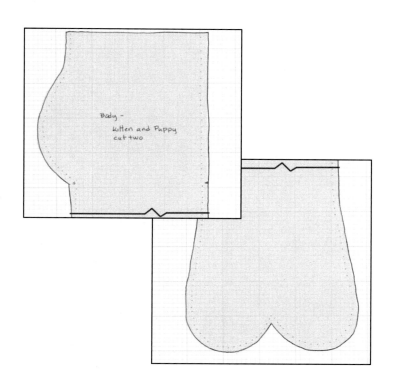

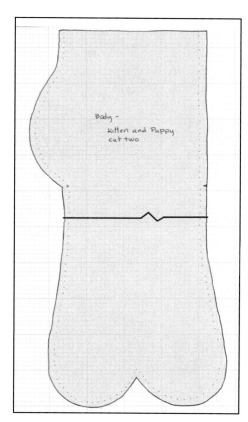

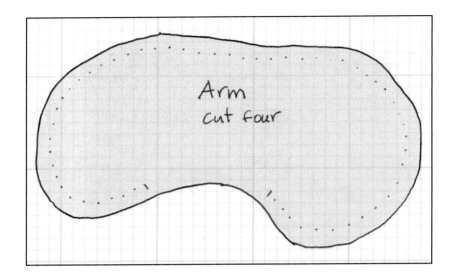

Arm
cut four

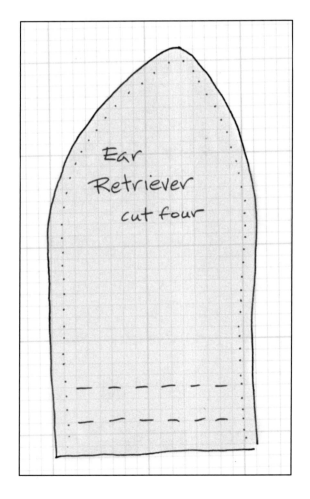

Ear
Retriever
cut four

kitten ear
cut four

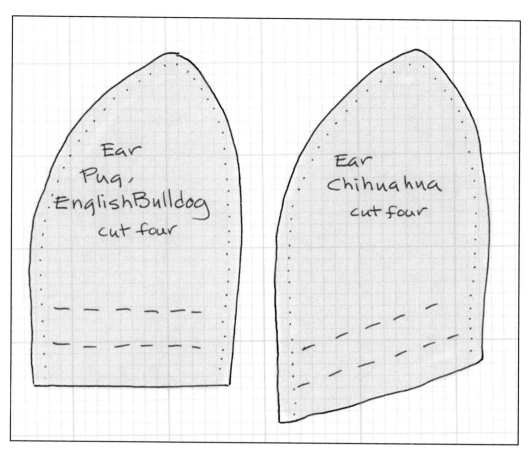

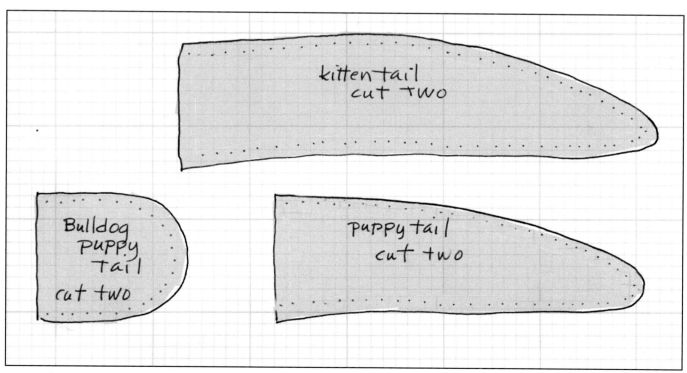

Ear - Rabbit
cut four

84

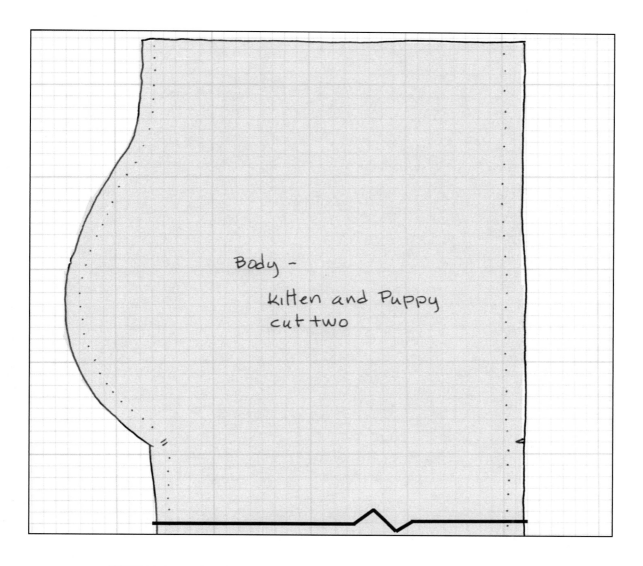

Body -

Kitten and Puppy
cut two

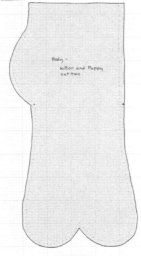

Join the body pattern above to the pattern on page 86. The joined pattern should look like the one shown here.,

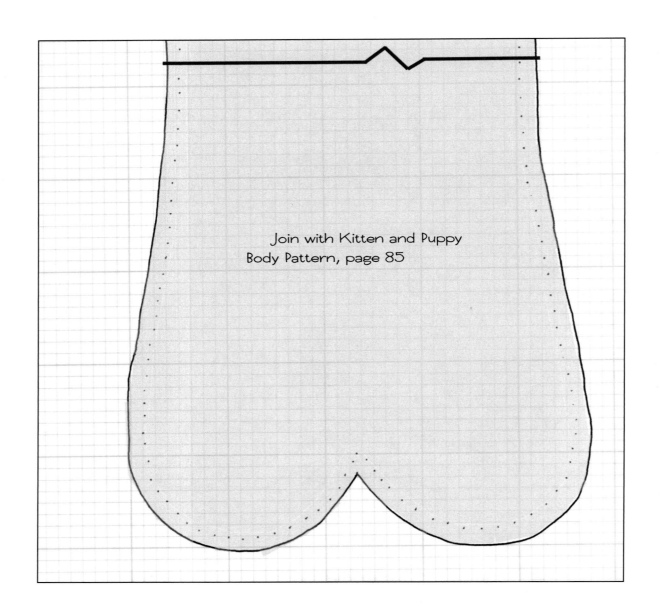

Join with Kitten and Puppy
Body Pattern, page 85

Join the bunny
body pattern on this
page with the lower
body pattern on page
88. The joined pat-
tern should look like
the one shown below.

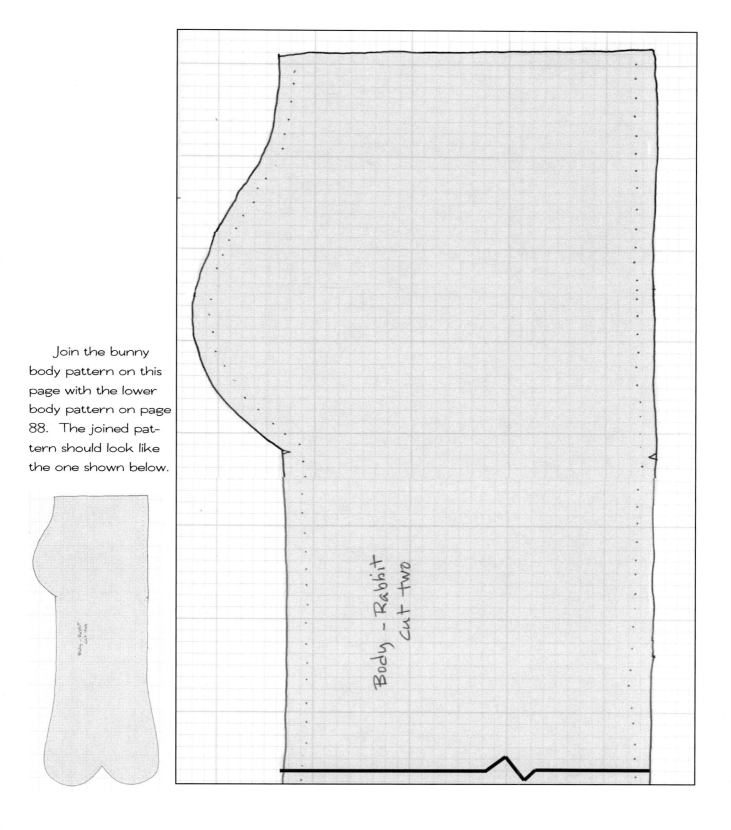

Body – Rabbit
Cut two

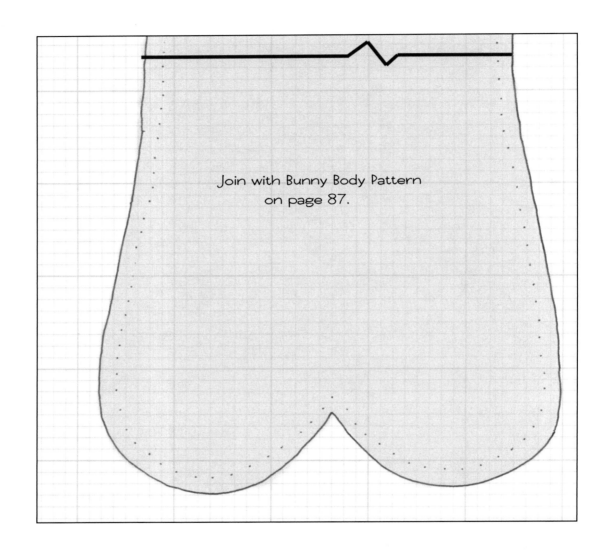

Join with Bunny Body Pattern
on page 87.

Clothes Patterns

Choose the patterns needed for the clothes you want to sew, and trace the patterns onto tracing paper. The playsuit pattern is too large to fit on one page, so join it together, as shown for the body on page 81. You may also want to make the playsuit legs longer than they appear here - I suggest an additional 1 ½ inch at the bottom of the pattern.

The only pieces that need to be fitted to the doll are the collar or yoke for the dress. You want the dress to cover the connection between the head and body. Since every doll head comes out a slightly different size, you may need to alter the pattern to make the neck opening to fit your doll.

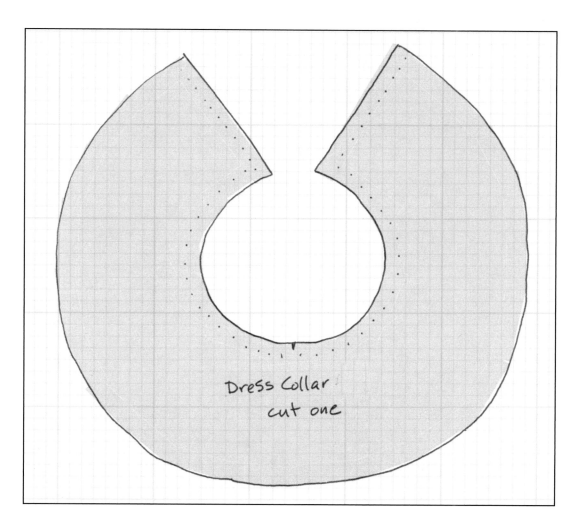

Dress Collar
cut one

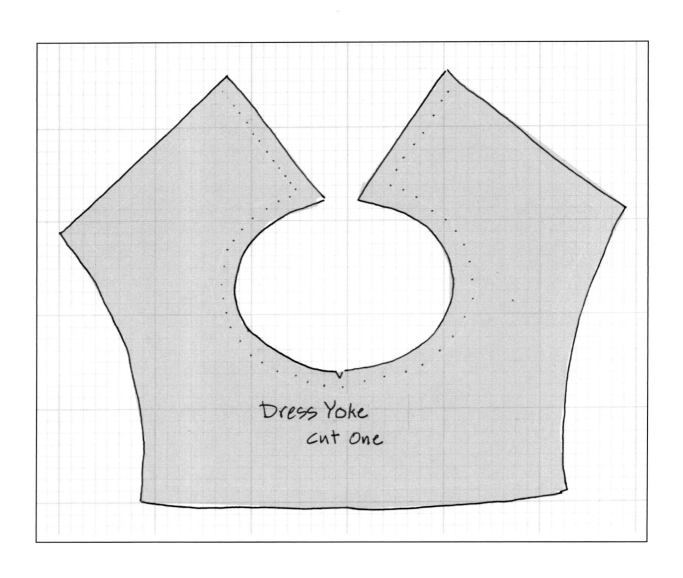

Dress Yoke
cut One

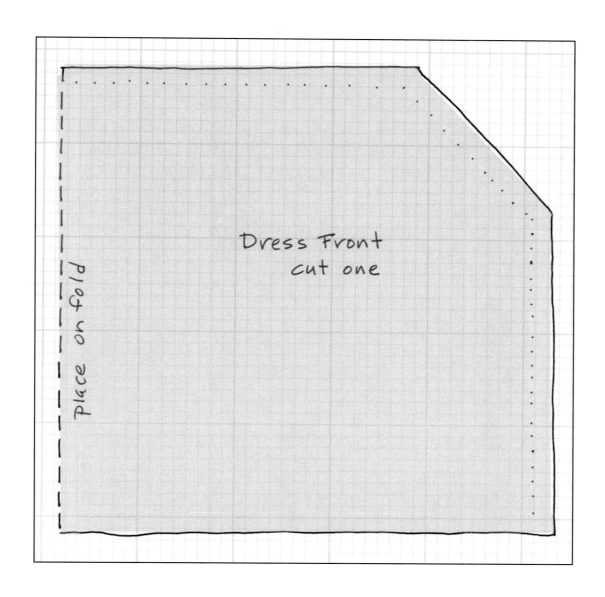

Place on fold

Dress Front
cut one

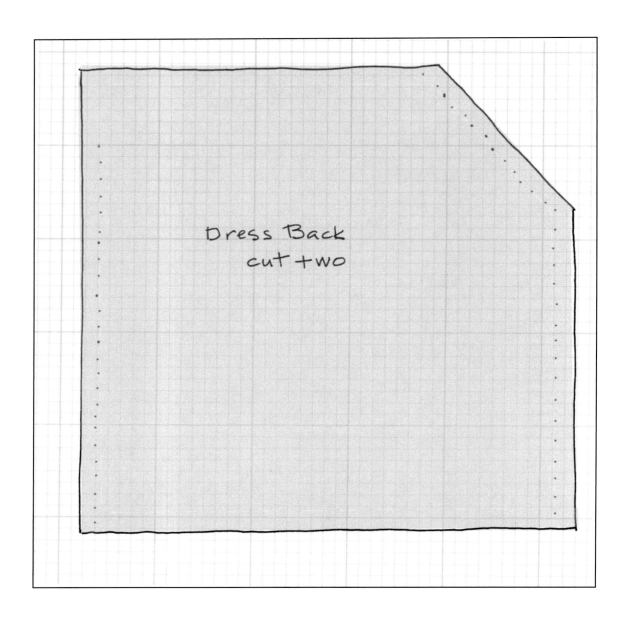

Dress Back
cut two

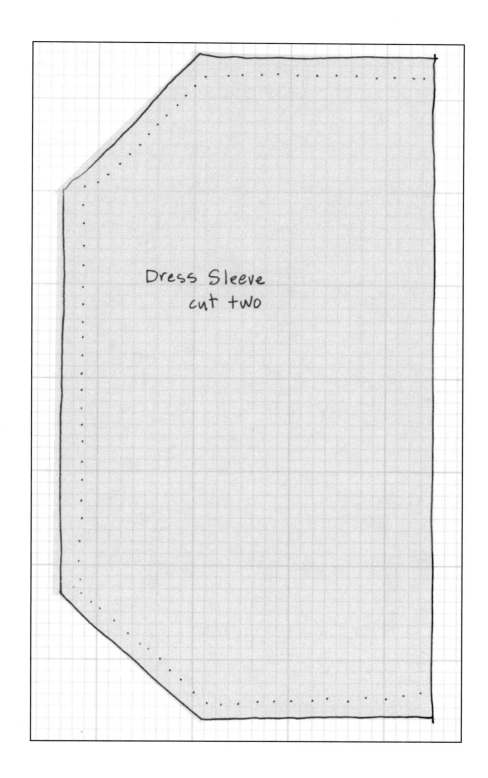

Dress Sleeve
cut two

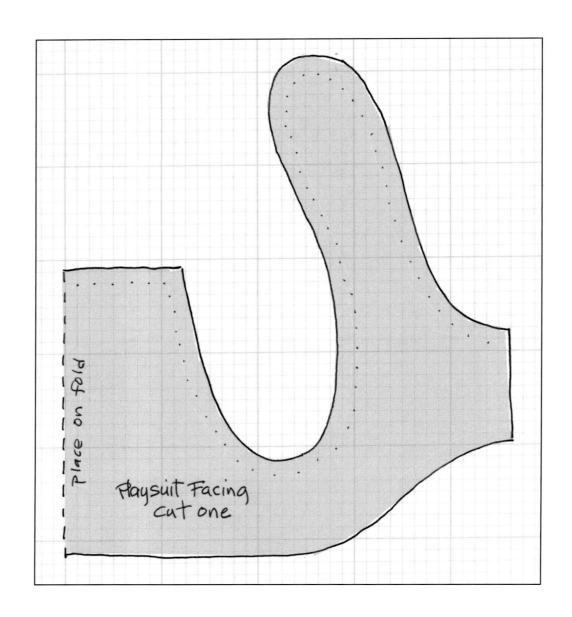

Place on fold

Playsuit Facing
Cut one

94

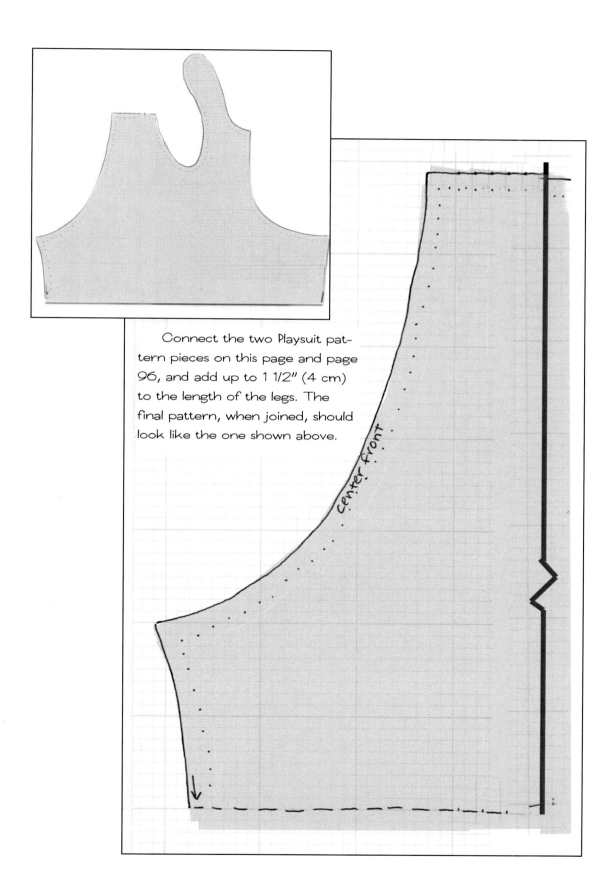

Connect the two Playsuit pattern pieces on this page and page
96, and add up to 1 1/2" (4 cm)
to the length of the legs. The
final pattern, when joined, should
look like the one shown above.

Center Front

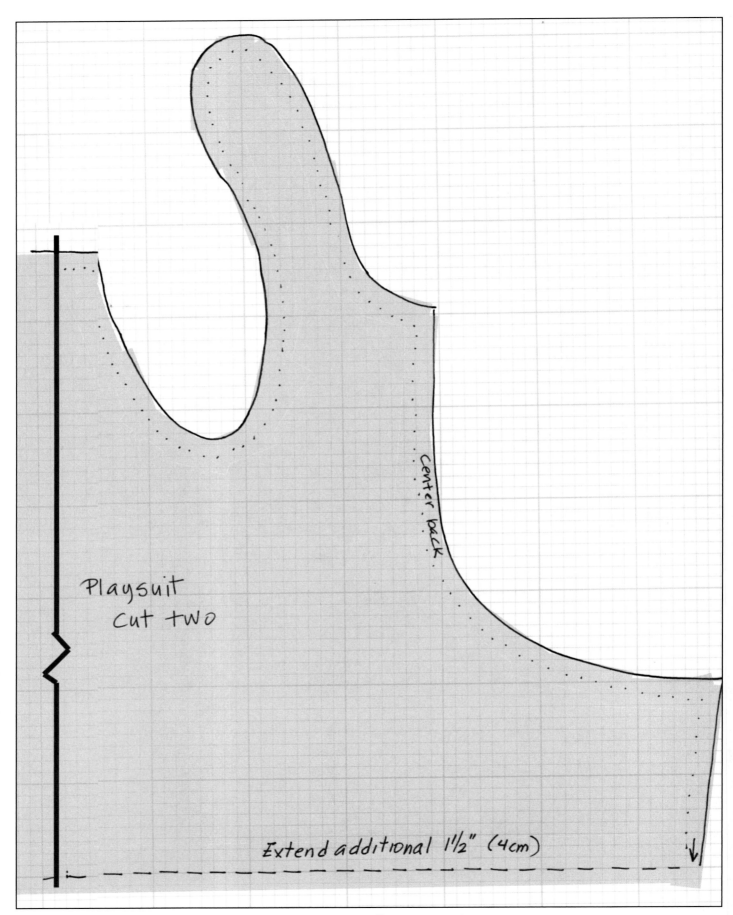

Playsuit
Cut two

Center back

Extend additional 1½" (4cm)

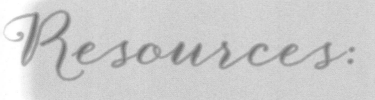

Resources:

Cotton Velour and Doll-Making Supplies:

I bought my velour, doll needles and wool stuffing
from WeirDollsAndCrafts.com

Dress Fabrics:

The pug's dress fabric was designed by Maudie&Ma, and it's available online at
SpoonFlower.com/profiles/maudie&ma

The calico cat, gray spotted bunny and golden retriever are wearing dresses made from fabric
designed by sharon Turner. Her fabric designs can be found at
SpoonFlower.com/profiles/scrummy

Don't forget that great doll clothes can be made with fabrics recycled from items you pick up at
the local thrift store.

I'll be adding more links and resources on my blog as they come to my attention. I've already made
two videos that may be helpful to you, on how to mix the air-dry clay, and how to sculpt the toes. I'm
always open to suggestions, so if you think other videos would be helpful, or if you have a site that you
think we should see—or even if you'd just like to come hang out with other creative people, please
come visit my website at UltimatePaperMache.com/dolls

27937634R00062